THE
EVERYTHING

Wedding
Checklist
Book

3RD EDITION

All you need to remember for
a day you'll never forget

Holly Lefevre

adamsmedia

Avon, Massachusetts

An Everything® Series Book.
Everything® and everything.com® are registered
trademarks of F+W Media, Inc.

Published by Adams Media, a division of F+W Media, Inc.
57 Littlefield Street, Avon, MA 02322 U.S.A.
www.adamsmedia.com

ISBN 10: 1-4405-0185-8
ISBN 13: 978-1-4405-0185-2
eISBN 10: 1-4405-0186-6
eISBN 13: 978-1-4405-0186-9

Printed in the United States of America.

10 9 8 7 6 5 4

Library of Congress Cataloging-in-Publication Data
Lefevre, Holly.
The everything wedding checklist / Holly Lefevre. — 3rd ed.
p. cm.
Rev. ed. of: The everything wedding checklist : the gown, the guests,
the groom, and everything else you shouldn't forget / Janet Anastasio
and Michelle Bevilacqua ; with Leah Furman and Elina Furman. 2000.
Includes bibliographical references and index.
ISBN 978-1-4405-0185-2 (alk. paper)
1. Weddings—Planning. 2. Wedding etiquette. I. Anastasio, Janet. Everything wedding checklist. II. Title.
HQ745.A53 2011
395.2'2—dc22
2010038516

This book is available at quantity discounts for bulk purchases.
For information, please call 1-800-289-0963.

Acknowledgments

I would like to thank the following people whose encouragement, insight, and guidance made this book possible: Amberly Finarelli at Andrea Hurst Literary Management for bringing this project to me; Katrina Schroeder at Adams Media for her guidance and for answering all of my questions; and all the vendors and brides I have worked with, who have taught me so much and inspired me.

Contents

Introduction

Congratulations on your engagement. Share the good news, break open the bubbly, and bask in the glow of being a bride-to-be, because you will soon be jumping headfirst into the exciting task of planning your wedding. Make no mistake, there'll be a lot to remember and a lot to do, and at times it may seem overwhelming, but don't fret. *The Everything® Wedding Checklist Book, 3rd Edition* is here to guide you through your planning.

When should you start looking for your wedding gown? How do you come up with a guest list? What are you supposed to do at the reception? What should you pack for the honeymoon? Yes, planning a wedding is filled with questions, but with this book you won't need to worry about where to find the answers. Within these pages, you'll find the answers you need, and a convenient place to stay on task and to keep track of names, appointments, and other pertinent information.

Whether it's picking a reception site, finding a photographer, choosing flowers, or any of the other million items on your checklist, this book can tell you when, where, and how to do them. The year-long planning calendar will put you on the right track and the subsequent checklists for each section will help you stay there. In addition, each chapter contains insights and advice on every aspect of your wedding, from hiring a wedding planner to seating the guests at the wedding to leaving on your honeymoon.

As unromantic as it may sound, sticking to a schedule and staying on task is the best and only way to ensure the planning goes smoothly. Brides tend to procrastinate in the early months, thinking that "a year is so far away." One year or eighteen months, or whatever your engagement time frame is, will fly by. So, don't wait. Besides, wouldn't you rather be free to enjoy basking in the glow of your position as a bride-to-be instead of being bogged down by tasks that could have been done months ago? Starting early will give you breathing room, and allow you to take your time and make wise choices.

In short, if you need to be informed about it or reminded to do it in order to plan your ultimate wedding, this book won't let you down.

General Thoughts

While you are planning your fabulous wedding, there are a few policies you should adopt to ensure that everything goes smoothly. These are relatively simple tips and strategies that can have a big impact on your wedding planning. Every bride can benefit from heeding the following advice:

- **Don't put off until tomorrow what you can do today.** There will be plenty to do as your wedding grows near; don't make things worse by leaving everything to the last minute.
- **Stick to your budget.** If you have a well-thought-out budget, life will be a whole lot easier. You won't end up in the poorhouse after your wedding, and you won't waste time pursuing options that you can't afford.
- **Get everything in writing.** Every aspect of every purchase or service agreement should be in writing, so if things don't work out to your satisfaction, you will have the proper recourse. Another way to keep from being a victim is to get references from every place you're considering doing business with.

Twelve-Month Wedding Planning Checklist

*A*fter the dust settles from the whirlwind of excitement and celebrations with family and friends, there are some things you'll have to do to get married. Depending upon the type and size wedding, you may have lots to do. In any event, the following schedule should give you a general idea of what has to be done, and when you should do it.

TEN TO TWELVE MONTHS
❏ Select an engagement ring
❏ Insure the ring
❏ Announce the engagement
❏ Set the date
❏ Attend your engagement party
❏ Hire a wedding planner
❏ Draft a preliminary guest list
❏ Draft a budget
❏ Begin a bridal registry
❏ Determine the style and formality
❏ Research a ceremony venue
❏ Research a reception venue
❏ Begin researching, interviewing, and hiring vendors
❏ Set up a wedding website

EIGHT TO TEN MONTHS

- ❑ Select the wedding party
- ❑ Select a ceremony venue
- ❑ Select a reception venue
- ❑ Shop for your gown
- ❑ Book a caterer (if necessary)
- ❑ Book entertainment
- ❑ Book a photographer
- ❑ Book a videographer
- ❑ Order Save-the-Date cards

SIX TO EIGHT MONTHS

- ❑ Order your wedding gown
- ❑ Book the florist
- ❑ Book a hairstylist
- ❑ Book a makeup artist
- ❑ Order the wedding cake
- ❑ Hire an officiant
- ❑ Secure rentals
- ❑ Organize travel accommodations for guests
- ❑ Organize accommodations for wedding night (and night before)
- ❑ Schedule an engagement photo session (after hiring photographer)
- ❑ Research wedding invitations
- ❑ Research honeymoon destinations and check travel advisories
- ❑ Finalize remaining vendor commitments
- ❑ Book parking attendants
- ❑ Order bridesmaids' dresses
- ❑ Research other stationery needs (menu cards, place cards, ceremony programs)

FOUR TO SIX MONTHS

- ❑ Mail Save-the-Date cards
- ❑ Select formalwear for the groom and men
- ❑ Have mothers shop for attire
- ❑ Plan the rehearsal dinner
- ❑ Plan the prewedding and postwedding parties
- ❑ Finalize the guest list
- ❑ Order the wedding invitations and announcements
- ❑ Order invitations for the rehearsal dinner and the wedding parties

- ❑ Hire a calligrapher for invitations and place cards
- ❑ Book the honeymoon
- ❑ Get your passports (if necessary)

TWO TO FOUR MONTHS
- ❑ Select wedding day transportation
- ❑ Shop for wedding bands
- ❑ Research marriage license requirements
- ❑ Research and select a seamstress for alterations
- ❑ Select the wedding favors
- ❑ Determine a reception menu
- ❑ Finalize cake flavors and design
- ❑ Shop for bridal accessories (lingerie, jewelry, headpiece/veil, etc.)
- ❑ Shop for bridesmaids' accessories (jewelry, shoes, purses)
- ❑ Develop a preliminary itinerary for the wedding day
- ❑ Verify the gown delivery date
- ❑ Address and assemble invitations
- ❑ Have the invitations weighed at post office, buy postage for the invitations and response envelopes
- ❑ Confirm delivery dates for wedding gown and bridesmaids' dresses

ONE TO TWO MONTHS
- ❑ Mail the invitations (six to eight weeks)
- ❑ Shop for thank-you gifts (attendants, parents, etc.)
- ❑ Prepare a shot list for the videographer and photographer
- ❑ Make arrangements for preserving the bridal bouquet
- ❑ Make arrangements for preserving your bridal gown
- ❑ Have a wedding day hair and makeup preview
- ❑ Finalize rehearsal dinner plans
- ❑ Send rehearsal dinner invitations
- ❑ Finalize the ceremony details
- ❑ Finalize the reception details
- ❑ Finalize musical selections with entertainment
- ❑ Attend dress fittings/alterations
- ❑ Prepare the wedding announcement for the newspaper
- ❑ Attend wedding showers
- ❑ Purchase wedding accessories (guestbook/pen, ring pillow, etc.)
- ❑ Schedule final beauty/grooming appointments

ONE MONTH

- ❏ Get a marriage license
- ❏ Finalize the itinerary with vendors and ceremony/reception locations
- ❏ Begin a seating plan for the reception
- ❏ Pick up the wedding bands
- ❏ Schedule the final gown fittings and confirm a pickup date
- ❏ Write thank-you notes (for any wedding gifts already received)
- ❏ Break in your wedding shoes
- ❏ Begin finalizing the wedding day itinerary

TWO WEEKS

- ❏ Give the final guest count to the caterer/reception location
- ❏ Call guests who have not responded
- ❏ Confirm the rehearsal dinner guest count
- ❏ Begin packing for the honeymoon
- ❏ Make final payments to vendors (payments due between now and the wedding day)
- ❏ Finalize the seating chart and send seating/place cards to calligrapher
- ❏ Prepare a "Bridal Emergency Kit"

ONE WEEK

- ❏ Pick up your gown
- ❏ Attend the final grooming/beauty appointments
- ❏ Call/e-mail venues and all vendors to finalize arrangements, delivery times, etc.
- ❏ Attend bachelor/bachelorette parties
- ❏ Arrange to have mail/package delivery stopped (during your honeymoon)
- ❏ Attend the bridal luncheon

TWO TO THREE DAYS

- ❏ Pick up the tuxedos for groom and men
- ❏ Cut checks for the remaining vendor payments
- ❏ Prepare vendor tips
- ❏ Drop off wedding accessories at the venue or to the wedding planner
- ❏ Deliver welcome baskets
- ❏ Pack a bag for the wedding day

ONE DAY

- ☐ Attend the ceremony rehearsal and distribute wedding day itinerary
- ☐ Deliver remaining accessories to the wedding planner, church coordinator, etc.
- ☐ Attend the rehearsal dinner
- ☐ Present attendants with their gifts at the rehearsal dinner
- ☐ Go to bed early—get your rest!

THE WEDDING DAY

- ☐ Give vendor tips and payments to best man or wedding planner
- ☐ Marry the man you love and have a great day!

AFTER THE WEDDING

- ☐ Send your bouquet for preservation
- ☐ Send your gown for cleaning and preservation
- ☐ Complete and mail the thank-you cards
- ☐ Thank your vendors (phone call and/or note)
- ☐ Thank your parents and attendants (phone call and/or note)
- ☐ Change your name, if you planning on doing that

CHAPTER 1

Ready, Set, Plan!

*I*n the blink of an eye, a simple question can transform your life. Your calendar transforms from business meetings and date nights with your sweetie to shopping for wedding rings and interviewing wedding planners. Although planning a wedding is fun and exciting, it can seem overwhelming and stressful at times. However, with a little organization, guidance, and most important, a plan, your wedding will be a once-in-a-lifetime experience.

The Ring

The ring. You have dreamed about it, looked for it, and waited for it. As with all other aspects of a wedding, selecting an engagement ring is accompanied by a myriad of questions, ideas, and expectations. A little research will help you make an informed decision about this important purchase.

Shopping Tips

Your first step in the search should be to consult a reputable jeweler. Rely on your own experiences or on referrals from family and friends to find one. If that doesn't yield many results, pick a store that appeals to you, stocks jewelry in your price range, and is a member of the American Gem Society. No matter where you begin your search, avoid taking any chances by following this advice:

- Stay open to all options. Even if you fall in love with the first ring you see, comparing selections from other jewelers will give you a better idea of fair pricing and other options. Beware of salespeople who pressure you to buy on the spot.
- Make the final sale contingent upon taking the ring to an appraiser of your choice. There's nothing rude about this course of action; unscrupulous jewelers may try to convince you to buy a ring for much more than its worth by having their appraiser (or one they recommend) "confirm" the ring's inflated value.
- Get a purchase agreement that includes stipulations for sizing and a potential return. Does the store offer a money-back guarantee if the ring is returned within the designated time frame? Does the agreement include any sizing, tightening, or cleaning? Some stores provide these services free of charge for a limited time.
- Get a written appraisal and insurance. It's not romantic, but you must get a written appraisal that describes the ring and cites its value for insurance purposes. Insure your ring under your homeowner's or renter's policy.

The Four Cs

The four Cs are the four marks of a diamond's quality. If you and your fiancé have set your sights on a diamond engagement ring (or, for that matter, if you plan to purchase a diamond wedding band), make sure you know the four Cs before forking over any of your hard-earned savings. The stone you purchase should pass the test in these four categories:

1. **Clarity:** The clarity is measured by the number of a diamond's flaws or imperfections (either interior or exterior). Broadly speaking, this is the most important factor in determining the beauty of a given stone: a stone with low clarity, for example, will have a number of imperfections when viewed under a gemologist's magnifying glass.
2. **Cut:** The cut is the stone's physical configuration, the result of the process that shapes the rough gem. The diamonds you will see at a jewelry store have many cuts on the surface of the stone to shape them and emphasize their brilliance. Common shapes include round (or brilliant), pearl shaped, oval, and marquise.

3. **Color:** The color is also a major factor in determining a diamond's value. Colorless stones are considered perfect. The object, then, is to find a stone that is as close to colorless as possible, unless, of course, you'd rather have color. (Many people prefer to wear stones with a slight discoloration, even though these stones are not worth as much as their higher-quality, colorless counterparts.)

4. **Carat:** The diamond's carat weight refers to the actual size of the stone. (Unlike the carat weight of gold, the carat weight of a diamond is simply a physical measure and not a measure of quality or purity.) Carat weight alone is not necessarily an indicator of price or value. A three-quarter-carat colorless, flawless diamond will almost certainly be appraised higher than a two-carat weight stone with several flaws and a murky, yellowish tint.

CHOOSING YOUR ENGAGEMENT RING

Jewelry store: _____

Address: _____

Telephone number: _____

Sales representative: _____

Store hours: _____

Notes: _____

_____

_____

ENGAGEMENT RING TABLE

Stone:	#1	#2	#3
Jewelry store:			
Clarity:			
Cut:			
Color:			
Carats:			
Other stones (if applicable):			

Setting _____

Notes: _____

_____

_____

Price per carat: _____

Tax, other charges: _____

Total price: _____

Final selection (stone number): _____

Ring size: _____

Order date: _____ Date ready: _____

Deposit amount: _____ Due date: _____

Balance: _____ Due date: _____

Notes: _____

_____

_____

The Wedding Date

At the first sight of an engagement ring on your finger, the questions will start. Although the first thing you're likely to hear is "Congratulations!" it will be followed closely by "When's the date?" You won't be able to forge ahead with other planning until you set a date; it is *the* essential element in all your wedding planning. When will you need the ceremony and reception sites? How long do you have to find a dress? When will you require the services of paid professionals, such as caterers, photographers, and musicians? These and many other questions will remain unanswered until you've set a date.

Determining Factors

In the preliminary search for a wedding date, be flexible; work with a season or month rather than one particular date. Then, look at your schedules and surroundings. Is a particular time of the year busy at work? Is summertime in your city just too hot to have an outdoor wedding? These circumstances may affect your decision. Once you examine the pros and cons of these factors, as well as the answers to the following questions, possible dates will fall into place.

- What season do you prefer? Do you want a country garden wedding in the spring? A seaside wedding in the summer? A celebration at a refurbished farmhouse in the fall? Does the season matter at all?
- Is there a time of year that your family or the groom's family finds particularly meaningful?
- How much time do you need to plan the wedding?
- Does the availability of a ceremony and reception site coincide with your desired date? If you have your heart set on a certain venue, it may already be booked for your particular day, and you may need to be flexible with the actual date.
- Are there conflicts for you, your family, or attendants (such as another wedding, a vacation, a graduation, a pregnancy/birth, military commitments)? It's doubtful your matron of honor would enjoy standing beside you in her eighth month. By the same token, your parents are unlikely to appreciate having to choose between your wedding and your brother's high school graduation.
- Consider the impact holidays, religious celebrations, and community events may have on your wedding. On a holiday weekend, guests may encounter crowds and more expensive travel accommodations. During religious holidays, the house of worship may not be available and some guests may be unable to attend.
- Check with the local parks and recreation department, chamber of commerce, community calendar, and the venue to make sure a major event is not scheduled in the same place on the same day. Annual events that draw large crowds or require street closure will also impact your plans.

Popularity by Month

During peak wedding months, there may be a lot of competition for services from flowers to frosting. Here's the breakdown of what percentage of marriages take place each month:

January: 3 percent
February: 2 percent
March: 4 percent
April: 7 percent
May: 11 percent
June: 13 percent
July: 10 percent
August: 11 percent
September: 12 percent
October: 17 percent
November: 6 percent
December: 4 percent

Announcing Your Engagement

The good news of your engagement will spread like wildfire. Before that happens, start off on the right foot with everyone. Follow the traditional protocol when announcing your engagement:

- Tell the bride's parents first.
- The groom's parents are told next.
- If your parents are divorced, tell the parent who raised you (or your fiancé), and then share the news with the other parent.
- Once all of the parents are privy to the engagement, the groom's parents should contact the bride's parents and, if possible, set up a meeting.
- If either the bride or groom has children, tell them immediately so they do not feel excluded in the process of combining the families.

Start Spreading the News

Publishing a formal announcement in the newspapers of your hometown and the city in which you live is a great way to spread the word. Most newspapers have standard announcement formats that include the names and occupations of the bride, groom, and their parents, schools attended, and possibly a photograph. Check with your local publication for details. Here is an example of a standard published announcement:

Engagement Announcement

Mr. and Mrs. (bride's parents) of (city, state) announce the engagement of their daughter, (bride's first and middle name), to (groom's full name), son of Mr. and Mrs. (groom's parent's names) of (city, state). A (month/season) wedding is planned. (Or, No date has been set for the wedding.)

Hear Ye, Hear Ye

At one time it was standard protocol for the hosts of the wedding to mail a printed formal engagement announcement. It is not standard practice today, but it does add a level of formality to the wedding plans. Formal engagement announcements are traditionally sent by the bride's parents, but they can also be sent by the couple or whoever is hosting the wedding. Be sure to include the following details on your printed engagement announcement:

- ❑ Hosts of the wedding
- ❑ Names of bride and groom
- ❑ Location of the wedding (city, state)
- ❑ Do not include the date or times (yet)

Wedding Planners

Lives today are busy enough with careers and social lives. The prospect of planning a wedding often leads to increased stress and anxiety. Even if you have the time to spare, planning a wedding involves a bit of research. An experienced wedding planner can show you the ropes and offer a tremendous amount of guidance.

Types of Wedding Planners

A wedding planner's purpose is not to take over the plans (unless that's what you hire her to do!), but rather to guide you through the planning process, offer creative ideas and time-saving techniques, and organize all of the aspects of the wedding day. To accommodate the range of needs and budgets represented by today's bride and groom, wedding planners offer an assortment of services. Not every wedding planner offers every type of service. The following general descriptions should help you understand the basics of planning services:

- **Full-service planner:** This service works with the couple from the beginning of the planning, but he may be called in at any point during the planning. In brief, the planner can assist with budgeting, finding and selecting venues and vendors, running wedding-related errands, and following up on all of the details. She is the bride's point person from start to finish. A full-service wedding planner may also assist with event design and styling aspects of the wedding.
- **Month-of planner:** This service may be hired at any time (earlier is better to ensure you get to work with the planner you want), but she typically begins her essential work one to two months prior to the wedding day. The planner offers referrals early in the planning and then organizes and fine-tunes your plans as the day draws nearer. She will manage the final wedding details, such as calling the vendors and creating an itinerary. She will also be present at the rehearsal and on the wedding day to ensure things are running smoothly and on time.
- **Day-of planner:** This service assumes and expects the bride to plan her wedding, finalize all the details and logistics, and create her own itinerary. The planner will then use the information the bride has provided to direct the rehearsal and guide the couple through the wedding day.
- **Hourly services:** If you could use the services of a wedding planner in some areas, but you are not interested in hiring someone to be with you on the wedding day, many planners will meet on an hourly basis.

Fees for wedding planners vary. Some planners charge a flat rate, others ask for 10 to 20 percent of the total cost of the wedding, and some charge by the hour. A planner's experience, expertise, and geographical location influence fees. Most planners are willing to customize their services to accommodate your specific needs. Finally, remember you are hiring a wedding planner to work for you. While you may be working with a location manager at your venue, this is not your wedding planner.

Questions to Ask

The days of wedding planners taking over and making your wedding theirs are over. Select someone who listens to your needs and ideas, and who is capable of handling the job. Ask friends, family, and coworkers for referrals. Consult the advertising pages of regional bridal magazines, the "Local Resources" section of popular wedding websites, or visit a local bridal show. Here is a list of questions that will help you find the right wedding planner:

- How long has the consultant been in business? (Many years in business should indicate experience and contacts. It also means that the person is probably reputable, as he or she hasn't been run out of town by unhappy clients.)
- Is the consultant full-time or part-time?
- Can you get references from former clients?
- Is the consultant a full-service planner, or does his or her expertise lie only in certain areas?
- If the consultant isn't a full-service planner, what services does he or she handle?
- Is the consultant affiliated with any organizations? What are they?
- Is the consultant scheduled to work with any other weddings that are on the same day as yours? (You don't want your consultant to be too busy with someone else to meet your needs.)
- How much (or how little) of the consultant's time will be devoted to your wedding?
- What is the cost? How is it computed? (Hourly? Percentage? Flat fee?)
- If the consultant works on a percentage basis, how is the final cost determined?
- Exactly what does the quoted fee include (or omit)?

Name: _____

Address: _____

Phone: _____

Contact: _____

Hours: _____

Appointments: _____

Date: _____ Time: _____

Date: _____ Time: _____

Date: _____ Time: _____

Date: _____ Time: _____

Date: _____ Time: _____

Service: _____

Number of hours: _____

Overtime cost: _____

Provides the following services: _____

Cost: _____

_____

_____

_____

_____

_____

Fee: Flat: _____ Percentage: _____ Hourly: _____

Total amount due: _____

Amount of deposit: _____ Date: _____

Amount due: _____ Date: _____

Gratuities included?   Yes   No

Sales tax included?   Yes   No

Date contract signed: _____

Terms of cancellation: _____

CHAPTER 2

Getting Down to Business

*W*eddings are a business, and when you are planning your wedding, you are the CEO of your wedding enterprise. It is your job to oversee vendors, crunch numbers, and manage tasks, all while keeping friends and family happy. It is a big job, but not an impossible one. With open communication, a plan, and some guidelines on how to deal with the business side, you can and will enjoy this experience.

Let's Talk Money

The "B-word," otherwise known as the budget, is the nasty little detail that no one wants to talk about. Your budget has a very big influence on your wedding. It will dictate the size and style of your wedding, as well as other aspects such as flowers, music, photography, video, transportation, and so on. As you determine your budget, remember that a wedding can be beautiful whether it costs $5,000 or $50,000. What will make your wedding memorable are the love and the people, not the elaborate extras.

The Budget

Talking money is not an enjoyable part of wedding planning, but it is a vital part of the process. Too often, couples sit down to sort out the wedding budget with no sense of what a wedding costs or what it takes to get them from A to Z. They have grand ideas, but no concept of how those ideas translate into reality, or how much those ideas cost. When it is time to set the budget, it is important to be realistic and to figure out *how* your wedding is going to be paid for.

Tips for Setting the Budget

1. Is anyone contributing monetarily—the groom, your parents, his parents? Honestly discuss your expectations and the finances with them.
2. Prioritize the areas of your wedding so that you can spend money on what's most important to you. Be willing to drop the notion of serving steak at the reception in order to afford a good photographer.
3. The date you select will affect your final costs. Prime or high-season wedding dates are from May through October.
4. Don't ignore your tastes. If you have grown up eating caviar at the finest restaurants, a cake and punch reception at the local community center is probably not going to satisfy you.

Traditional Expenses

While the bride's parents traditionally financed a major portion of the wedding, it is commonplace for the groom's parents to contribute to the budget. As couples marry later in life and have the financial means to do so, the bride and groom also finance a portion or sometimes the entire wedding. It is not uncommon for the groom's family to contribute as well.

TRADITIONAL BRIDAL EXPENSES:

- Bridal gown and accessories
- Invitations, reception cards, and announcements
- Fee for the ceremony site
- Flowers for the ceremony and reception
- Attendants' bouquets
- Bride's father's and grandfather's boutonnieres
- Music for the ceremony and reception
- Groom's wedding ring and gift
- Photography and videography
- Housing and gifts for the bridesmaids
- Limousines/transportation
- Reception costs (venue, food, liquor, and décor)

TRADITIONAL EXPENSES FOR THE GROOM AND HIS FAMILY:
- Bride's wedding and engagement rings
- Bride's bouquet and gift
- Marriage license
- Officiant's fee
- Corsages for the mothers and grandmothers
- Boutonnieres for the groom, groomsmen, his father, and grandfather
- Ushers' housing and gifts
- Rehearsal dinner
- Honeymoon

BRIDESMAIDS' EXPENSES:
- Their dresses and accessories
- A shower gift
- A bridal shower
- A bachelorette party (a portion of)
- Their travel expenses
- A gift for the couple

GROOMSMEN'S EXPENSES:
- Their tuxedos or suits
- A bachelor party
- Their travel expenses
- A gift for the couple

Working with the Pros

On the wedding day, all of your carefully laid plans are in the hands of your vendors. The vendors you hire and the relationships you establish with them plays a major role in the success of the wedding. If you look in the right places, you will find qualified, reliable vendors who will meet your needs.

Finding the Right Ones

Vendors, if chosen wisely, are your greatest wedding day allies. Professional and reliable vendors are available in all areas and for all budgets. Researching their qualifications and making sure you and the vendor have a good rapport in terms of personality and style are important steps in ensuring wedding day success. You can begin your search for wedding vendors in the following places:

- The Internet is a great place to search for local vendors. From major, national websites, you can find links to local professionals. The websites of professional wedding organizations include referrals to their members. Don't forget to check out local website and bridal blogs.
- Regional bridal publications cover the professionals and local happenings in their region. They also contain advertisements for vendors in all categories.
- Bridal shows are a great place to meet vendors. You can see samples of their work and get an overall impression of their style and demeanor.
- Referrals from friends and family members are a great way to get leads. If you know someone whose judgment you trust, relying on his or her feedback about a vendor is particularly helpful.
- You may also get referrals from vendors, venues, and your wedding planner. Referrals from qualified professionals you have hired or trust are definitely worth a look.

Signing on the Dotted Line

Interview each vendor thoroughly. Search the Internet for reviews; unhappy brides tend to find a way to make themselves heard. Ask each vendor for references, but keep in mind that a vendor is not going to give you the phone numbers of people who are unhappy with his or her services. Finally, remember that advertisements are placed by the vendors, so of course they are going to be glowing endorsements. Once you find the professional you are happy with, get a written contract.

CONTRACT CHECKLIST
- ❏ Date of the event
- ❏ Time of the event
- ❏ Arrival/Set up time of the vendor
- ❏ Name of the company
- ❏ Name of the person/persons performing the service (if applicable)
- ❏ Attire/Dress code (if applicable)

❏ Location/Locations of the event
❏ Detailed description, including the type and scope of services to be performed
❏ Any specialized or extra services or provisions discussed, such as thematic attire
❏ Deposit information: how much and when it is due
❏ Payment information: how much and due dates
❏ Cancellation policies
❏ Signatures of both parties

Tipping

Even the most thorough couples often overlook one very substantial expense—tips! Depending on the tone and formality of your wedding, tipping can easily add from a few hundred to a few thousand dollars to your costs. Although tipping is, for the most part, expected, it is never required, and it is solely at your discretion. A tip, for extraordinary service, is always a welcome surprise, and if you decide to tip after the wedding, that is fine, too. If you cannot afford to tip, a glowing letter of recommendation and the offer to be a reference is always appreciated.

How to Tip

As if you didn't already have enough to remember for your wedding day, now you need to add tipping to the list? With some preplanning, tipping your wedding professionals is simple and easy. Just follow these steps:

❏ Predetermine the tipping amounts by taking into account the level of service the vendor has provided thus far; it is a good indication of the level of service you can expect on the wedding day.
❏ Consult the tipping guidelines for an idea of typical tipping amounts. Take into account the locale of your wedding and the formality; high-end venues equal high-end tips.
❏ Place each vendor's tip in an envelope that is clearly marked with the vendor's name.
❏ At the rehearsal, rehearsal dinner, or the morning of the wedding, pass the envelopes off to the wedding planner, best man, or the designated point person. Ask this person to distribute the tips at the conclusion of each vendor's service.

Tipping Guidelines

The tipping guidelines that follow are guidelines, not rules. Exactly how much or whom you tip is completely at your discretion. Many of the guidelines offer percentages, but flat fees are okay, no matter what the amount. Always check your contracts and paperwork, because some wedding professionals include a gratuity in their contract.

- Some caterers and reception site managers have gratuities of 15 to 20 percent included in their contracts (some don't, just ask). Their tips are usually paid in advance by the host. If the caterer or manager has been exceptionally helpful, you may wish to give her a tip, usually $1–$2 per guest.
- The banquet captain runs the venue's portion of the reception. He oversees all of the food and beverage service, and sees that the guests are comfortable and happy. He should be tipped approximately $1–$5 per guest depending on the location.
- Waitstaff usually receive 15–20 percent of the food bill or $10–$20 per server. Caterers sometimes include this gratuity in their contract. If the tip was not paid to the caterer in advance, give the tip to the head waiter/maitre d'/banquet captain during the reception.
- A wedding planner is paid a fee for her service, but if your planner has provided exceptional service and care during the planning and on the wedding day, a tip is in order. Ten percent of their fee or anywhere from $50–$500 is acceptable.
- Bartenders should be tipped in the range of $50–$100. The location and size of your wedding should determine the amount. For example, a bartender for a small wedding at a moderately priced restaurant would fall in the $50 range, while a bartender at a wedding for 200 guests at an expensive hotel should be tipped more in the $100 range.
- Restroom, coat check, or parking attendants should be prepaid by the host, usually $1–$2 per guest or car. You may ask the staff not to accept tips from guests.
- Limousine drivers receive 15–20 percent of the bill. This tip is almost always included in the contract. Any additional tips are at the host's discretion.
- Musicians or DJs may be tipped if their performance was exceptional. Tips usually run about $25 per musician. DJs are tipped in the range of $50–$200. The level of service and scale of the wedding will determine the final amount.

- Florists and bakers are usually not tipped; you simply pay a flat fee for their services. If you do choose to tip, 15 percent is standard.
- Photographers and videographers are often not tipped. Of course, you can always tip if you want to. This amount, anywhere between $50–$250, would depend on how pleased you are with the service provided by the photographer and the overall scale (budget) of your wedding
- Delivery personnel or setup staff receive $5–$20 each.
- Makeup artists and hairstylists should be tipped 15–20 percent of their bill.
- A hired officiant receives a flat fee for performing the service. A tip of $50–$200 could be in order. The actual amount would depend on the length and details of the ceremony, as well as the amount of time and care he or she spent with you prior to the wedding. A religious officiant usually asks for a donation to his or her house of worship. This ranges from $50–$500 and is typically outlined when you book the house of worship, or you may ask the officiant or venue coordinator for customary amounts. A civil officiant, like a judge, is not allowed to accept tips.

✄ WEDDING BUDGET WORKSHEET

Item	Projected Cost	Deposit Paid	Balance Due	Who Pays
WEDDING CONSULTANT				
Fee				
Tip (usually 15–20%)				
PREWEDDING PARTIES				
Engagement (if hosted by bride and groom)				
Site rental				
Equipment rental				
Invitations				
Food				
Beverages				
Decorations				
Flowers				
Party favors				
Bridesmaids' party/luncheon				

Item	Projected Cost	Deposit Paid	Balance Due	Who Pays
Rehearsal dinner (if hosted by bride and groom)				
Site rental				
Equipment rental				
Invitations				
Food				
Decorations				
Flowers				
Party favors				
Weekend wedding parties				
CEREMONY				
Location fee				
Officiant's fee				
Donation to church (optional, amount varies)				
Organist				
Tip (amount varies)				
Other musicians				
Tip (amount varies)				
Program				
Aisle runner				
BUSINESS AND LEGAL MATTERS				
Marriage license				
Blood test (if applicable)				
WEDDING JEWELRY				
Engagement ring				
Bride's wedding band				
Groom's wedding band				
BRIDE'S FORMAL WEAR				
Wedding gown				
Alterations				
Undergarments (slip, bustier, hosiery, etc.)				
Headpiece				
Shoes				
Jewelry (excluding engagement and wedding rings)				
Purse (optional)				

✿✿ WEDDING BUDGET WORKSHEET—continued

Item	Projected Cost	Deposit Paid	Balance Due	Who Pays
Makeup artist				
Hairstylist				
Going-away outfit				
Going-away accessories				
Honeymoon clothes				
GROOM'S FORMALWEAR				
Tuxedo				
Shoes				
Going-away outfit				
Honeymoon clothes				
GIFTS				
Bride's attendants				
Groom's attendants				
Bride (optional)				
Groom (optional)				
RECEPTION				
Box or pouch for envelope gifts				
Champagne				
Decorations				
Dessert				
Entrées				
Equipment rental (chairs, tent, etc.)				
Guest book and pen				
Hors d'oeuvres				
Liquor				
Meals for hired help				
Nonalcoholic beverages				
Party favors				
Place cards				
Printed napkins				
Servers, bartenders				
Site rental				
Tip for caterer or banquet manager				
Tip for servers, bartenders				
Toasting glasses				

WEDDING BUDGET WORKSHEET—continued

Item	Projected Cost	Deposit Paid	Balance Due	Who Pays
Wine				
Wine service for cocktail hour				
PHOTOGRAPHY AND VIDEOGRAPHY				
Album				
Engagement portrait				
Extra prints				
Mother's albums				
Photographer's fee				
Videographer's fee				
Videotape				
Wedding portrait				
Wedding prints				
Wedding proofs				
RECEPTION MUSIC				
Musicians for cocktail hour				
Tip (optional)				
Live Band				
Tip (optional)				
DJ				
Tip (optional)				
FLOWERS AND DECORATIONS				
Boutonnieres				
Bride's bouquet				
Bridesmaids' flowers				
Cake table				
Corsages				
Decorations for reception				
Decorations for wedding site				
Flowers for reception site				
Flowers for wedding site				
Head table				
Lighting for ceremony				
Lighting for reception				

WEDDING BUDGET WORKSHEET—continued

Item	Projected Cost	Deposit Paid	Balance Due	Who Pays
Potted plants				
Table centerpieces				
WEDDING INVITATIONS AND STATIONERY				
Announcements				
Calligrapher				
Invitations				
Postage (for invitations and response cards)				
Save-the-Date cards				
Thank-you notes				
WEDDING CAKE				
Wedding cake				
Groom's cake				
Cake top and decorations				
Flowers for cake				
Cake serving set				
Cake boxes				
WEDDING TRANSPORTATION				
Limousines or rented cars				
Parking				
Tip for drivers				
GUEST ACCOMMODATIONS				
GUEST TRANSPORTATION				
HONEYMOON				
Accommodations				
Meals				
Spending money				
Transportation				
ADDITIONAL EXPENSES (LIST BELOW)				
TOTAL OF ALL EXPENSES				

CHAPTER 3

The Honor of Your Presence

*I*f you're like most brides, compiling your guest list can be challenging—unless, of course, you have an open-ended budget and unlimited reception space. Not only do you need to figure out who is going to make the cut, but you also need to decide who is going to have a say in the process, and on top of it all make the list manageable enough to stay within the budget without sacrificing the guest's comfort or your style.

Who's on the Guest List

For the important and possibly delicate task of determining who is invited to the wedding, work with your fiancé and families to create a guest list that suits your wedding plans. If you are like most brides, you will need to make hard decisions, as will your fiancé and your families. So, when it is time to tackle the guest list, follow these simple steps and establish some guidelines to get you moving on the right path.

Dividing the Guest List

In most cases the guest list is divided evenly between the families, regardless of who is paying for what, with the bride's parents, the groom's parents, and the couple each inviting one-third of the guests. The next step is to list everyone you'd ideally like to have, so you can see if the total number is beyond your reach.

Setting Boundaries

If the guest list is too long, establish some boundaries to trim it down. Just remember, you must apply all rules across the board. Making exceptions for certain people is the single best way to offend others and create more headaches for yourself. You may want to consider implementing any or all of the following policies:

- **No children.** The fact that you're not inviting children is indicated to parents by the fact that their children's names do not appear anywhere on the invitation. Just to be safe, however, make sure your mother (and anyone else who might be questioned) is aware of your policy. What age you choose as a cutoff point between children and young adults is up to you.
- **No coworkers.** If you were inviting people to the wedding to strengthen business ties, this may not be the best option, but if you do need to cut somewhere, and you feel comfortable excluding work acquaintances, this may be the way to go.
- **No thirds, fourths, or twice-removeds.** If you have a large immediate family, you may want to exclude distant relatives, with whom you have no regular social interaction.
- **No "and Guest."** While you will certainly want to allow any "attached" guests to bring their significant others, the same does not necessarily need to extend to unattached guests. In other words, if you're on a tight budget and some guests are not part of an established couple, they can go stag and hang with the rest of the swinging singles. If you can't afford to invite single guests with a date, they will almost certainly understand. Remember, however, that married and engaged guests must always be invited along with their spouses and fiancés. Likewise, each of your attendants should be given the option to bring a guest, even if they're not involved in a relationship.
- **No return invitations.** If a distant relative or acquaintance invited you to his or her wedding, you do not automatically have to return the favor. They will understand if you make them aware that you're cutting costs and having a small affair. However, if your wedding is on a grand scope with an already large guest list, returning the invitation may be appropriate, or you may have some explaining to do.
- **Be honest with the "not-invited."** If people approach you and assume they're being invited when they're not, be honest with

them—and quickly. Waiting only serves to make the situation even more awkward. Tell them you'd love to have them, but it's impossible to invite everyone on your wish list.

- **No regrets.** Because it's realistic to anticipate some regrets (on average, about 20–25 percent of invited guests will be unable to attend), you and your fiancé may decide to send a second mailing of invitations to people on your B-list. It has become popular for couple to have an A-list and a B-list. The B's receive invites as the A's decline the invitation. If you need to make cuts, forgo the B-list invites. However, if you choose to do two mailings, the first should be sent eight to ten weeks before the wedding date; the second should be sent out no later than five weeks prior.

Making the List

Once you start making the guest list, make sure to stay organized. You must be thorough and complete when collecting the invitation information. There is nothing worse than a guest receiving an invitation with their names misspelled, or having your beautiful invitations returned "Address Unknown."

Information Confirmation

Check to make sure that the following information is correct before mailing any invitations. If you're not 100 percent sure on any point, ask someone who would know, or ask the person in question. Collect all of the proper information for each guest and record it on the Wedding Guest Checklist that follows, so that when it comes to invitation time, you are ready to go!

- ❏ Spelling of names
- ❏ Titles (doctors, military personnel, etc.)
- ❏ Addresses
- ❏ Names of significant others
- ❏ Phone numbers (just in case you need to call a late responder, or if any of your friends or family want to contact guests to invite them to showers or other parties in your honor)

WEDDING GUEST CHECKLIST

RSVP	NAME	ADDRESS
☐	1.	
☐	2.	
☐	3.	
☐	4.	
☐	5.	
☐	6.	
☐	7.	
☐	8.	
☐	9.	
☐	10.	
☐	11.	
☐	12.	
☐	13.	
☐	14.	
☐	15.	
☐	16.	
☐	17.	
☐	18.	
☐	19.	
☐	20.	
☐	21.	
☐	22.	
☐	23.	
☐	24.	
☐	25.	

WEDDING GUEST CHECKLIST

RSVP	NAME	ADDRESS
❑	26.	
❑	27.	
❑	28.	
❑	29.	
❑	30.	
❑	31.	
❑	32.	
❑	33.	
❑	34.	
❑	35.	
❑	36.	
❑	37.	
❑	38.	
❑	39.	
❑	40.	
❑	41.	
❑	42.	
❑	43.	
❑	44.	
❑	45.	
❑	46.	
❑	47.	
❑	48.	
❑	49.	
❑	50.	

✿ WEDDING GUEST CHECKLIST

RSVP	Name	Address
❏	51.	
❏	52.	
❏	53.	
❏	54.	
❏	55.	
❏	56.	
❏	57.	
❏	58.	
❏	59.	
❏	60.	
❏	61.	
❏	62.	
❏	63.	
❏	64.	
❏	65.	
❏	66.	
❏	67.	
❏	68.	
❏	69.	
❏	70.	
❏	71.	
❏	72.	
❏	73.	
❏	74.	
❏	75.	

✤ WEDDING GUEST CHECKLIST

RSVP	NAME	ADDRESS
❏	76.	
❏	77.	
❏	78.	
❏	79.	
❏	80.	
❏	81.	
❏	82.	
❏	83.	
❏	84.	
❏	85.	
❏	86.	
❏	87.	
❏	88.	
❏	89.	
❏	90.	
❏	91.	
❏	92.	
❏	93.	
❏	94.	
❏	95.	
❏	96.	
❏	97.	
❏	98.	
❏	99.	
❏	100.	

Welcoming Ways

Since your long-distance friends and relatives will be coming a long way for your reception, try to make things as pleasant and convenient for them as possible. Travel information, activities, and a welcome basket upon their arrival make a grand impression and make them feel truly welcome. There are some very simple steps you can take now to make their trip as easy as possible.

Accommodations

Shortly after you get engaged, make arrangements for group rates with the airlines and hotels. Send this information to your guests with the Save-the-Date card, as a separate mailing, or post it on your wedding website. Prepare a travel package with all the phone numbers, websites, and other vital information that the guests will need to plan their trip. Here are a few pointers for keeping the guests happy:

- Always check to see whether your preferred hotels will offer a lower rate for a group of rooms. Grouping out-of-town guests in one hotel has several advantages: the group rates will lighten the burden on their pockets; they can mingle with the other guests during the downtime between wedding events; and they can carpool to and from the festivities.
- Help the out-of-towners find a place to hang their hats over the course of their stay, whether with family members, friends, or local hotels. Provide the guests with hotel information. Generally, guests pay for their own lodging (unless either the bride's or groom's family can offer to pick up the tab).
- Include several lodging options, detail the prices and any special features of each place, and tell the guests where you're attempting to coordinate group rates. This way you're assuming nothing about your guest's financial situation.

Ways to Welcome

Once the guests have made the commitment and put forth the effort to be a part of your wedding festivities, show your appreciation with some of these hospitable gestures:

- Finances permitting, have a bottle of wine or a welcome basket delivered to the guests upon their arrival at the hotel room.

- Provide a letter or packet containing all the pertinent wedding information, as well as information on local attractions and maps of the area.
- If possible, invite the out-of-towners to your rehearsal dinner. If this is not possible, schedule a welcome party or gathering (it doesn't have to be an over-the-top soiree). Many couples also plan a postwedding brunch before sending the guests off. Be sure to include an itinerary for the weekend's events, so that the out-of-towners know what other wedding events are scheduled to take place while they're in town.
- Enclose detailed maps to all the events for those unfamiliar with the area. You don't want guests who have traveled across country to make it to your wedding only to miss the event because they got lost a few miles from the ceremony site.
- Consider providing transportation to and from the wedding ceremony and reception. Then put a trustworthy friend or relative in charge of rounding up the out-of-town group and transporting them from place to place. This person would also be in charge of airport pickups and dropoffs.
- For those out-of-town guests who are bringing children along for the ride, talk about finding a babysitter well in advance. (Some churches have babysitters on hand.) Children who are not going to the ceremony/reception can still be invited to the rehearsal dinner.

CHAPTER 4

The Write Stuff

*T*he wedding invitation is a guest's first glimpse into your wedding festivities. The invitation ensemble you select speaks volumes about the tone, style, and formality of your big day. But it is by no means the beginning or end of the paper trail. Save-the-Dates, menu cards, and wedding programs are key components of your stationery wardrobe. So, whether you select elegant and engraved or one-of-a-kind customized creations, make sure your selections give the guests the right impression.

Save-the-Date Cards

Save-the-Date cards let guests know a wedding is being planned for a particular date, giving them enough time to clear their schedules. These cards should be sent at least six months before the wedding date. If you are planning a destination wedding, live in a resort town, are planning a wedding during peak travel times, or know many of your guests plan their travels twelve months out, sending Save-the-Date cards earlier is always acceptable.

Creating the Save-the-Date Card

There are a couple of points to keep in mind. First, this card is a preview of your wedding; therefore, its formality and tone should reflect the overall tone of your event. Second, the card is not an invitation to anything; it is merely a precursor to the invitation, giving the guests time to make travel arrangements, so be sure to send those invitations when the time is right. Although the Save-the-Date conveys basic wedding facts, many couples choose to include more detailed travel, tourist, and accommodation information so that guests may begin planning their trip.

The basic Save-the-Date wording is simple.

❑ Bride's and groom's name
❑ The host's name (optional)
❑ Date of the wedding
❑ Geographic location of the wedding (a specific venue is not necessary yet, but at least the city or state where the wedding is being planned)

Save-the-Date Sample

Save the Date
for the marriage of
Julie Nelson
and
Arthur Wood
June 25, 2012
Los Angeles, California
Formal invitation to follow

Invitations 101

At first, ordering a wedding invitation might sound simple, and although it can be quick and easy, the options for creating this wedding masterpiece are quite varied. There are typestyles, ink colors, printing options, paper weights, and more to consider when selecting your wedding invitation.

Ordering your invitations from four to six months in advance (it all depends on the printing and details) will allow enough time for the invitations to be printed, received, assembled, and addressed. Custom-designed invitations will require more time for the design process. Finally, always ask to see a proof (sample) of everything so you can proofread for typos and incorrect information before approving the final printing.

Be sure to order an extra set of invitations and envelopes. Invitations are typically sold in increments of twenty-five to fifty, and it is much less expensive to order a set or two now, rather than later. Having to place an order of just twenty-five (or fifty) invitations after the original order has been placed will incur the same charges as a first-time order; tacking them onto the original order is much less expensive. You will also need extra envelopes to account for any mistakes you may make when addressing them.

Here is a list of the basic information you should know as you begin researching wedding invitations:

- What is the overall style and formality of the wedding? (Your invitations should reflect this.)
- How many invitations do you need? You can usually count one invitation per household.
- How will you word your invitation? Will your parents' names appear on the invitation? What about your fiancé's parents? Will you be using a poem or verse or other unique wording?
- Confirm and reconfirm the details. Be sure you have the correct ceremony start time, the correct spellings of all people and locations, the address for the ceremony and reception.
- When is your response deadline? It is usually two to three weeks prior to the wedding. If you are using an RSVP service, you will need the company's designated phone number and website information.
- Are you providing guests with a meal choice? You will need to indicate the choices on the response card.

Printing Methods

There are four main printing options to consider when shopping for wedding invitations.

1. Engraving is the most formal and one of the most expensive options. A metal plate of the invitation is made and the paper is pressed onto it, raising the print, on which a layer of ink is then printed.
2. Letterpress is the reverse process of engraving; a plate is pressed into the paper from on top, leaving the letters depressed into the card. These invitations are fairly equivalent in price to engraved invitations.
3. Thermography is an extremely popular and cost-effective option that offers a similar look to engraving. Ink and powder are fused

together to give the letters a raised appearance on the front of the invitation.

4. Lithography or offset printing is a flat printing process that is the least expensive option.

If you are having fifty guests or fewer, it is acceptable for the invitations to be handwritten (although few brides do this, as there are so many cost-effective options). If you choose this route, use your best handwriting or find a friend with beautiful handwriting to reflect the occasion.

Components

The components of the basic wedding invitation include:

- The invitation, which invites the guest to the wedding and provides the necessary details; bride's and groom's name, host, date, time, and ceremony location.
- The response card and envelope, which allows the guests to indicate whether they'll be attending and if they're bringing a guest (if a guest is invited). If you are offering a choice of entrées, you may also need to include space for the guest's entrée selection.
- The reception card, which directs the guests to the location of the reception. If the ceremony and reception are in the same location, a reception card is not always necessary. You may print "Reception immediately follows" in the lower left corner of the invitation.
- The map or direction card, which provides guests with the address and driving directions to the wedding venue/venues.
- The inner envelope was part of a traditional presentation, but it is often skipped to save paper. The stacked and completed invitation ensemble is inserted into the inner envelope with the text facing the back flap.
- The outer envelope contains the complete invitation, whether inserted into the inner envelope or stacked on its own. Print the return address on the back flap, and then stamp and mail this outer envelope.

INVITATION INFORMATION

Stationer/Printer: _____

Address: _____

_____

Phone: _____

Contact person: _____

Number of invitations: _____

Delivery date: _____ Price: _____

Get Them in the Mail

Once you have received your beautiful wedding invitations, it is time to assemble them and send them on their way. The invitations should be mailed approximately eight weeks before the wedding, with an RSVP date of about three weeks before the wedding. If you're planning a wedding near a holiday, mail your invitations a few weeks earlier to give your guests some extra time to plan.

Address for Success

Before you can get started on the invitations, you must have the proper equipment, and some knowledge of what it takes to properly address your invitations. Here are some simple tips and guidelines to help you. Before you know it, the responses will be pouring in.

NECESSITIES FOR ADDRESSING THE INVITATIONS:
- Several black pens
- Friends or family members with good penmanship, or the services of a professional calligrapher
- A complete guest list with proper names and addresses
- Stamps, including the proper postage for the invitation, and a stamp for the response card
- Invitations and envelopes

Follow these standard guidelines when addressing the invitations:

- Use black ink.
- Address the invitations by hand, whether that is by you, a friend, or a professional calligrapher. Many couples also use computer-generated calligraphy directly on the envelope, which is acceptable depending on the formality of your wedding. However, peel-and-stick labels are considered a faux pas.
- If several people are helping you, be sure the same person addresses the sets (i.e., the inner and outer envelopes should have matching penmanship).
- Always address people formally as Mr., Mrs., Ms., Miss, or Master.
- With the exception of Mr., Mrs., and Ms., do not use abbreviations.
- Decide if you will take a formal or slightly more casual approach. A formal approach would read "Mr. and Mrs. Joseph Andrew Jackson" on the outer and "Mr. and Mrs. Jackson" on the inner envelope. A less formal approach would read "Linda and Joseph Jackson" on the outer envelope and "Linda and Joseph" on the inner envelope.
- For a married couple with different last names, each person's full name should be on a separate line, with the woman's name listed first. The same holds true for an unmarried couple living together. For a same-sex couple, list the names alphabetically.
- For an entire family, the parents' names are on the outer envelope, and their children's names are added to the inner envelope descending by age order.
- Never connect two names with "and" unless the two people are a married couple. If the names are too long to fit on one line, indent the second name under the name on the first line.
- Never put either "and guest" or "and family" on the invitation, the former is considered rude and impersonal, while the latter denotes the invitee's entire family (cousins, in-laws, etc.).

Pack Them Up and Ship Them Out

When your wedding invitations arrive from the printer, they may seem like a big puzzle. You may be wondering, "What am I supposed to do with all of this?" The pieces are there, but how do they fit together? This task may seem daunting, and slightly overwhelming at first, but you will quickly see that if you're organized, you will be done in no time.

Most wedding invitations require extra postage, either for weight or for size regulations; therefore, be sure to assemble one sample invitation and take it to the post office to be weighed for correct postage. This will avoid the return of your beautiful invitations for insufficient postage. Here are specific guidelines for assembling your invitations:

1. Place a response card, face-up, under the flap of the response card envelope. Be sure the envelope has the proper postage affixed.
2. Place the tissue over the lettering on the invitation. (Tissue is not necessary, and in fact, many companies no longer include it. Even if your invitations come with the tissue, you don't have to use it.)
3. The invitation is stacked from the largest piece on the bottom (usually the invitation) to the smallest piece on top. Begin by stacking the inserts on top of the invitation in descending order from largest to smallest.
4. Insert the invitation face-up into the inner envelope, which already has the guests' names written on it.
5. Insert the inner envelope into the outer envelope with the hand-written names facing the back of the envelope.

Programs, Menus, and Place Cards, Oh My!

A complete wardrobe of fine stationery will provide a special touch, show your attention to detail, and provide keepsakes from your magical day. Most of these printed items are optional, but they may assist the guests in their visit or in their enjoyment of the wedding day.

Stationery Checklist

Here are some other stationery items you may wish to include in your stationery wardrobe:

❏ Announcements
❏ At-home cards
❏ Boxes for the groom's cake
❏ Ceremony cards (if your ceremony is in a public place)

- ❏ Ceremony programs
- ❏ Coasters
- ❏ Cocktail napkins
- ❏ Favor cards/tags
- ❏ Matchbooks
- ❏ Menu cards
- ❏ Name cards (to let the world know if you are taking your husband's name, hyphenating your name, or retaining your maiden name)
- ❏ Pew cards/Within the ribbons cards
- ❏ Place cards
- ❏ Rain cards (to notify guests of alternate plans in case of rain)
- ❏ Table numbers/names
- ❏ Thank-you cards
- ❏ Welcome letters/itinerary for guests

CHAPTER 5

What's Your Style?

*T*o plan your wedding properly, you have to decide on the type of wedding you want. Although you may be eager to get moving on the fun stuff—interviewing musicians, sampling caterers' cuisine, viewing banquet halls, and trying on wedding gowns—figuring out your wedding style first will be time well spent and will help guide you through the many decisions yet to come.

Formally Speaking

The formality of your wedding will govern almost all aspects of your planning. The budget, size of the guest list, and time of day greatly influence the formality of the wedding as well. The following are some general guidelines to follow. Just remember, whatever level of formality you choose, try to keep it more or less consistent throughout.

Levels of Formality

Acquainting yourself with the traditional hallmarks of formality will assist you in deciding the tone for your wedding. For modern weddings, there is a great deal of emphasis on making each event unique and personal. As this trend continues, the lines between "very formal," "semiformal," and "informal" are blurring.

A VERY FORMAL WEDDING:

- Occurs in a church, synagogue, preferred house of worship, or luxury hotel
- Two hundred or more guests

- Engraved invitations with traditional typeface and wording
- Floor-length bridal gown, cathedral-length train, full-length veil, and long sleeves/arm-covering gloves
- Cutaway or tails for the groom
- Four to twelve bridesmaids and a matching number of groomsmen
- Matching floor-length bridesmaids' dresses or gowns
- Matching cutaways or tails for the groomsmen
- Formal attire (white tie for evening) for the guests
- A luxury hotel, event space, private club, private mansion, or other unique property for the reception site
- Elaborate sit-down dinner
- Orchestra or live band
- Elaborate floral and event design
- Hired transportation, such as limousines or antique cars

A FORMAL WEDDING:
- Occurs in a church, synagogue, preferred house of worship, or luxury hotel
- One hundred or more guests
- Engraved or letterpress invitations with traditional wording
- Floor-length bridal gown, chapel-length or sweeping train, finger-tip veil or hat, and gloves
- Cutaway or tails for the groom
- Three to six bridesmaids and a matching number of attendants
- Matching floor-length bridesmaids' dresses or gowns
- Matching cutaway or tails for groomsmen
- Formal attire or evening wear (black tie for evenings) for guests
- A luxury hotel, event space, private club, private mansion, or other unique property for the reception site
- Sit-down dinner, buffet, or stations
- Live band or disc jockey
- Medium-size bouquets and floral displays
- Hired transportation such as limousines, antique cars, or horse-drawn carriages

A SEMIFORMAL WEDDING:
- Held in a church, synagogue, preferred house of worship, hotel, outdoors, or other inspiring location
- Fewer than one hundred guests

- Thermography invitations printed with traditional or personalized wording
- Floor- or cocktail-length bridal gown with a fingertip veil or hat
- A tuxedo, sack coat, or suit and tie for the groom
- One to three bridesmaids and a matching number of attendants
- Matching floor- or cocktail-length bridesmaids' dresses
- Matching tuxes or suits and ties for groomsmen
- Evening or business dress for guests
- a hotel, event space, club, garden, restaurant, or home for the reception site
- A simple meal, light refreshments, hors d'oeuvres
- Live band or disc jockey
- Small bouquet for the bride, simple flower arrangements for decorations

AN INFORMAL WEDDING:
- Daytime ceremony often held at home or in a judge's chambers
- Fewer than fifty guests
- Printed or handwritten invitations with personalized wording
- A simple bridal gown, suit, or cocktail-length dress, with no veil or train
- A dark business suit and tie for the groom
- One attendant each
- A street-length dress for the maid-of-honor (or matron)
- A suit and tie for the best man
- Reception at home, at the site of the ceremony, or at a restaurant
- A simple meal or light refreshments
- Corsage or small bridal bouquet, simple flower arrangements for decorations

Defining Your Formality

There are many other factors to consider when determining the level of formality you want for your wedding. You may also want to take into account some of the following personal factors when determining your wedding's formality:

- **Lifestyle.** If you grew up eating caviar and drinking champagne, will a simple reception at the church hall satisfy you and your guests, or visa versa?

- **Personality.** If you are casual in your everyday life, would holding a very formal wedding make you feel like a princess or like a fish out of water?
- **Locale.** Does your dream of marrying barefoot on the beach "marry" with your other dream of dinner and dancing at a five-star hotel? Or, for example, if you dream of marrying with the ocean as your backdrop, you may need to schedule an afternoon or daytime wedding depending on the time of year. If the sun sets prior to the ceremony, no one will even see the ocean. You may have to compromise on some of your ideas based upon the formality and locale.

To Theme or Not to Theme

What could be more fun than selecting flowers, linens, lighting, and finding inspiration for other special touches for your wedding? If you are like most brides, you have been looking forward to this aspect of the planning. When designing your wedding, remember the theme should work with your locale and the formality of your wedding, but most important, it should reflect your style. Your personality, interests, and creativity should guide you in designing the wedding of your dreams.

Selecting a Theme

A theme can make a wedding unique. You can explore your fantasies of living in another time or transport your guests to another place. When selecting a theme, look for inspiration in your everyday life: a favorite vacation destination, a favorite flower, a collection, a hobby, the season, or even the location of the wedding. If you throw a theme wedding, be sure to let the guests in on the plan. Part of the fun is for everyone to be involved. If your theme would be enhanced by the guests dressing the part, include information on costume shops in the Save-the-Date or in a separate mailing.

Here are some themes to think about:

- **Ethnic flare.** There's no better way to say "I'm proud of my heritage" than to orchestrate an ethnic-themed wedding. It is the perfect way to highlight the culture and costumes of your ethnic background.

- **Western bonanza.** This style includes everything from cowboy hats to fiddles, square dancing, horses, barbecue fare, and anything else that's associated with the wild frontier and the pioneer spirit.

- **Happy holiday.** Take advantage of the decorations and spirit of a particular holiday. Valentine's Day, with its emphasis on love and romance, is a popular wedding time; the winter holidays are also popular. Easter and Passover are less popular because of certain religious restrictions, but a patriotic motif, complete with fireworks, might be a great idea for the Fourth of July. Halloween weddings are popular, with the wedding party and guests coming in costume.

- **Movable feast.** Like to travel? In the progressive wedding variation, the bride and groom attend a number of wedding festivities carried on over a period of days—and located in different places! Depending upon your budget, your love of travel, and the availability of friends and relatives to celebrate, you might start with your ceremony on the Eastern Seaboard, have a reception in the Midwest, and wrap things up in California. (Not all progressive wedding celebrations are that far-flung; many stay in the same state, even the same city.)

- **Trip down Memory Lane.** Stroll down Memory Lane with your groom, family, and friends by having the wedding at a place of special significance to you as a couple. Perhaps you want to return to the college where you met or to the park where he proposed.

- **All-nighter.** This is a wedding celebration that's planned to last through the entire night. In some cases, the group rents an additional hall after the first reception. In others, the festivities continue at a private home. The wedding usually comes to a close with breakfast the next morning. Coffee, anyone?

- **Destination wedding.** Guests are invited to a romantic honeymoon-type locale such as a resort or an inn, where they can stay with the new couple for a few days. After wedding is over, the bride and groom depart for the real (and much more private) thing.

- **"Surprise! You're a wedding guest!"** The surprise wedding is a surprise for your guests. Invite people to a standard-issue party, and if those in the know can keep a secret, your guests will be completely surprised when they arrive at a wedding.

- **No frills.** After all these grand suggestions, it's easy to forget that sometimes the most beautiful and enjoyable weddings are the ones that are the simplest. Without frills and thrills, the meaning of the marriage celebration becomes clearer, and you realize that no matter where you are, it is the people you're with who are important.

If after pondering some of these choices, a theme still doesn't appeal to you, relax. A theme is not necessary to create a memorable wedding. Many couples select a color or a small detail—such as a ribbon, flower, special motif, or a monogram—to style their event. Use one of these special items to carry out a consistent look by incorporating them into the various elements of the reception and ceremony.

Style Worksheet

If you are still trying to determine the theme or style of your wedding, jot down some basic dos and don'ts, likes and dislikes, and favorites, and you may begin to see your wedding style emerge. Also, comb through your bridal magazines and books. Certainly, you have earmarked pages that appeal to you. Pull all of these elements together along with the information on the following Style Worksheet and a style plan will begin to emerge.

Ideal ceremony (Description): _____

_____

Ideal reception (Description): _____

_____

Proposal location: _____

Favorite color/colors: _____

Favorite season: _____

Favorite flower/flowers: _____

Favorite pastime/hobby: _____

Special interests: _____

_____

_____

Going Green

"Going green" is a trend that is turning into a wedding staple. As everyone is becoming more aware of the impact of wastefulness on the planet and what it means for the future, brides are "showing their colors" by looking to avenues that promote recycling, repurposing, and reducing the economic and ecological footprint their wedding leaves behind.

The trend is growing; however, it still may be difficult to find vendors in all areas that are green. If you cannot find a green vendor, offer suggestions to the available vendors. For example, ask them to use locally grown and produced products and supplies. Of course, going green may not save you green, but it will help save the planet.

The Path to Green

Here are some ideas on making your wedding green. Work with your vendors and do a little footwork yourself to implement some of these concepts.

GOING GREEN CHECKLIST

- ❏ Work with a caterer or venue that promotes recycling.
- ❏ Ask your caterer and guests to recycle.
- ❏ Use locally grown organic produce and products.
- ❏ Use locally grown organic florals or, better yet, incorporate potted plants that can later be planted.
- ❏ Try paper-free invitations (use ones made from hemp or bamboo) or use 100 percent Post-Consumer Waste Recycled Paper and nontoxic inks.
- ❏ Serve organic wines.
- ❏ Have your favors reflect a green theme such as reusable shopping bags, stainless steel water bottles, tree seedlings, seeds, or organic fruits and nuts.
- ❏ For typically disposable items such as table numbers and escort/place cards, use organic or reusable products such as leaves, lemons, rocks, or items that are made from recycled paper.

CHAPTER 6

The Perfect Place

*I*t used to be easy—a wedding ceremony was held at the family church followed by a reception at the local hotel or in the church's community room. That was then; this is now. Today, a marriage is marriage, but a wedding is another thing entirely. Consequently, the choice of a wedding venue, both for the ceremony and reception, is one of the most important elements. It sets the tone for planning and plays a major role in all stylistic decisions.

The Ceremony Venue

Squaring away the details of your ceremony should be one of your first and highest priorities. If you don't know the location, time, and date of the ceremony, then you certainly can't do much to plan the reception. Try to get a ceremony date six to twelve months before you want the wedding to occur, particularly if you want a date between April and October. Competition for ceremony sites in those months can be pretty fierce, so you're more likely to get the day and time you want if you start looking early. If you don't plan on a long engagement, set the date as soon as you can.

Types of Ceremonies

One of your first decisions should focus on the tone and style of your ceremony. Here, you need to consider your views on religion and marriage. Your upbringing and your family's views may also influence this decision. You might want to acquaint or reacquaint yourself with the more common guidelines for wedding ceremonies. If you are not particularly religious or do not attend a regular church, examine some of the different types of ceremonies that are available to you. For more specifics regarding different types of religious ceremonies, refer to Chapter 12. Here are some points to consider when thinking about your ceremony venue:

- A civil ceremony is nonreligious. It is presided over by a civil or government official, such as a judge, justice of the peace, a hired officiant, or a legally able friend. It can be as formal and dramatic as traditional church weddings. You will need a marriage license, and you may need witnesses; each state has different requirements, so research what they are. If you opt for a civil or nondenominational ceremony, your particular house of worship may not recognize your union within its organization, although it is legally valid.

- A nondenominational ceremony emphasizes religion without being associated with any particular group. It is often free of the structure and restrictions of traditional religious ceremonies, but it does have a religious tone. The format of the ceremony typically resembles a traditional Protestant ceremony; however, customs and traditions from all religions may be blended into the ceremony. The reception venue, a boat, public spaces (i.e., a park, garden, or beach), and some nondenominational churches are all possible locations for the ceremony. This is a popular choice for couples who do not have a strong religious background, have different religious backgrounds, are marrying in a place other than a house of worship, or want the freedom to create their own ceremony.

- An interfaith marriage is between two people from different religions. Some religions will permit and recognize these unions, while some prohibit them and will not recognize the union. Interfaith ceremonies are usually held in religiously neutral locations. Many times, depending on the particular officiants involved, the ceremony may even be presided over by leaders from both the bride's and groom's religion. Not all officiants will agree to these terms, so if this is what you want, be sure to ask.

Questions to Ask

Here are a few questions you should ask as you scout location sites. Some questions may pertain specifically to houses of worship and should be discussed with the officiant.

- ❏ What kind of services does the facility provide (music, reception area)?
- ❏ What fees are required for marrying in the facility?
- ❏ What specifically do the fees include? Is there a security deposit?
- ❏ What is the cancellation or postponement policy?
- ❏ Will the facility provide any decorations? Carpeting? Aisle runner? Ribbon?
- ❏ Are there restrictions on décor?
- ❏ Are there any restrictions as to the kind of music you can have at the ceremony?
- ❏ Is a microphone or sound system available for the officiant?
- ❏ What are the rules regarding photography and video recording?
- ❏ Will you be dealing with a coordinator for the ceremony site over the course of planning the ceremony, or speaking directly with the officiant?
- ❏ Is there a bridal changing room?
- ❏ Are there any other weddings that day?
- ❏ Is there room to have receiving line at the back of the facility? What about outside, in a courtyard or garden?
- ❏ What is the parking situation?
- ❏ Is the site wheelchair accessible?
- ❏ Is the site air-conditioned?
- ❏ Is the site available for the rehearsal? At what time?

Ceremony Site Tracker

Use this handy checklist to keep track of the information on your venue options:

Ceremony Site: _____

Contact/Location manager: _____

Address: _____

_____

Phone number: _____

Website: _____

Notes: _____
_____
_____
_____
_____

Ceremony Site: _____
Contact/Location manager: _____
Address: _____
_____
Phone number: _____
Website: _____
Notes: _____
_____
_____
_____
_____

Ceremony Site: _____
Contact/Location manager: _____
Address: _____
_____
Phone number: _____
Website: _____
Notes: _____
_____
_____
_____
_____

The Reception Venue

After you secure a ceremony date and location, find a reception site. During peak wedding months (April–October) competition for sites is heavy; if you're marrying in this time frame, start looking at least a year in advance. During your search, keep in mind a couple of key factors:

1. **Proximity.** The proximity of the ceremony and reception venues to each other is important. The two locations should be

no more than a thirty-minute drive apart. You don't want your guests spending more time driving than enjoying your wedding celebration.

2. **Accessibility.** The accessibility of the site is also a key factor. There are many amazing places for a wedding, but you have to consider the guests' needs and their ability to arrive safely at the destination. For example, would you be crushed if your ninety-year-old grandmother couldn't make it down the rocky beachfront staircase to see you exchange vows? If so, pick another location.

Reception Options

When it comes to finding the perfect reception venue, the big question is "What are you looking for?" You need a site that fits into your budget, can hold all your guests, and still presents an appearance and atmosphere that you like. With any site you visit, notice the architectural details, color schemes, overall care and maintenance of the property, and photography sites. Does the setting suit the mood you want to evoke? How well would this site fit into your dream wedding?

If you'd like to get away from the traditional banquet hall reception, consider these alternatives:

- Aquarium
- Castle, estate, or historic mansion
- College or university
- Concert hall
- Country inn
- Historic hotel
- Lighthouses
- Museum or gallery
- Observatory
- Private or state park or garden
- Theater
- Yacht, ship, boat

Questions to Ask

During your meeting, make sure you receive satisfactory answers to the following questions. Often the information can be found in the site's brochure or literature, but the location manager should be able to provide any answers you need.

- ❑ Is the site conveniently located?
- ❑ What size party can the site accommodate?
- ❑ What rooms are available?
- ❑ How long is the site available? Is there a minimum amount of time? Are there overtime charges if the reception runs late?
- ❑ Is there a dance floor? (What size?)
- ❑ Does the site have a catering service? Can you bring in your own caterer if you wish?
- ❑ Does the site provide tables, chairs, dinnerware, and linens? What about decorations?
- ❑ Can the facility accommodate live music? Does it have the proper layout, wiring, and equipment?
- ❑ Does the site coordinator have any recommendations for setup and decorations? Can he or she recommend any florists, bands, disc jockeys, or caterers?
- ❑ Are there any restrictions regarding decorations, music, or photography?
- ❑ May you see photos of previous receptions?
- ❑ What services come with the site (i.e., waiters, waitresses, bar-tenders, parking valets)?
- ❑ What is the standard server-to-guest ratio?
- ❑ What kind of reservation deposit is required?
- ❑ Will there be any other weddings at the site on the same day as yours?
- ❑ Is there a package plan? Is so, what does it include?
- ❑ Are gratuities included in the price you quoted?
- ❑ Is there any rental fee for table linens, plants, decorations?
- ❑ Does the price vary with the time of day?
- ❑ If it is an outdoor site, what alternate plans are there in case of inclement weather?
- ❑ Will the deposit be returned if you have to cancel?
- ❑ Does the site have a liquor license? Liability insurance? Are you required to show proof of liability insurance?
- ❑ What is the policy on open bars? If you do have an open bar, are you responsible for providing the liquor?
- ❑ Is there a corkage fee? (If you're supplying your own liquor, some sites will charge a corkage fee to cover the costs of the staff opening bottles and pouring drinks.)
- ❑ What are the drink prices at a cash bar versus a hosted bar?
- ❑ What types of beverages are available?

- ❏ Is there an added price for garnishes for the bar?
- ❏ What is the layout of the tables? How many people does each table seat?
- ❏ Is there enough parking? Is it free? If there is valet parking, what is the policy on rates and gratuities?
- ❏ Is there a coat-check room? Will there be coatroom and rest-room attendants? A doorman? What are the charges?
- ❏ Are there changing rooms for the bride and groom?
- ❏ Who pays for any police or security that may be required?
- ❏ May you see their references?

Once you have solid answers to these questions, and after you've evaluated your needs and wants and have the facts and figures, you need to determine which site meets your needs and your budget. A deposit (usually a significant nonrefundable amount) will reserve the site you want. Be sure to get a written contract stipulating every term of your agreement (specific costs, details, inclusions, exclusions, special requests) before giving your deposit. Signing a contract will also protect you from becoming a victim of escalating fees, which come into play when you reserve a site well in advance of the wedding date. Perhaps you've reserved the site in August for a wedding the following August. If you don't sign a contract specifying this year's prices, the site may try to charge you new, higher rates.

Reception Site Tracker

Use this handy checklist to keep track of the information on your reception site options:

Reception Site: _____

Contact/Location manager: _____

Address: _____

_____

Phone number: _____

Website: _____

Notes: _____

_____

_____

_____

_____

Reception Site: _____

Contact/Location manager: _____

Address: _____

_____

Phone number: _____

Website: _____

Notes: _____

_____

_____

_____

_____

Reception Site: _____

Contact/Location manager: _____

Address: _____

_____

Phone number: _____

Website: _____

Notes: _____

_____

_____

_____

_____

Reception Site: _____

Contact/Location manager: _____

Address: _____

_____

Phone number: _____

Website: _____

Notes: _____

_____

_____

_____

_____

CHAPTER 7

Support System

*Y*our engagement brings excitement, not just to you, but to those closest to you. Involving your nearest and dearest as members of the wedding party is an honor. Whether it's your best friend, your future sister-in-law, your little sister, or your mother, these people have signed on to stick with you through the delights and frustrations of wedding planning. Just remember to surround yourself with supportive, loving people who will help make this a very special time in your life.

The Wedding Team

As soon as you and your fiancé decide out who you want to join the wedding party, ask them. There is a financial and time commitment involved, and it is best to give everyone enough notice to prepare for these commitments.

Keep in mind you want loving and supportive people around you. A wedding party is no longer about lining up the girls on one side and the boys on the other. There really are no strict rules anymore, as long as you use good judgment. The "new" wedding party includes those who are closest to you and those who are supportive and accepting and happy to be part of your special day—whoever they are.

Finally, the number of bridesmaids, groomsmen, and ushers you and your fiancé have is up to you, but in general, the more formal the wedding, the more attendants you have. The numbers do not have to be equal either. Don't ask your third cousin's daughter just because you need an extra bridesmaid; there are ways to work around uneven numbers.

Wedding Party Responsibilities

The wedding party should be made up of special people who want nothing more than your happiness. You should be able to lean on them for support because they have your best interests at heart. Be sure to consider the responsibilities that go along with each job. Make copies of these lists and hand them out to your would-be attendants to clear up any confusion they may have about their duties.

DUTIES OF THE MAID/MATRON OF HONOR:

- Helps the bride address envelopes, record wedding gifts, shop, and takes care of other prewedding tasks
- Arranges a bridal shower
- Helps the bride arrange her train and veil at the altar
- Collects funds and organizes a group gift to the bride
- Brings the groom's ring to the ceremony, and holds it until the ring exchange
- Holds the bride's bouquet as she exchanges rings with the groom
- Signs the marriage certificate
- Stands in the receiving line (optional)
- Makes sure the bride looks perfect for all the pictures
- Dances with the best man during the attendants' dance at the reception
- Participates in the bouquet toss, if single
- Helps the bride change into getaway clothes

DUTIES OF THE BRIDESMAIDS:

- Assist the bride and maid of honor with prewedding errands and tasks
- Help organize and run the bridal shower
- Assist the bride, in any way, on the wedding day
- Participate in the bouquet toss, if single
- Stand in the receiving line (optional)

DUTIES OF THE BEST MAN:

- Helps the groom get ready and arrive on time for every wedding-related function
- Drives the groom to the ceremony
- Brings the bride's ring to the ceremony site
- Gives the officiant his or her fee immediately before or after the ceremony (provided by the groom's family)
- Holds the bride's ring during the ceremony
- Escorts the maid of honor in the recessional
- Signs the marriage certificate as a witness
- Dances with the maid of honor during the attendants' dance at the reception
- Proposes the first toast at the reception
- Assists with distributing final payments and tips at the wedding
- Drives the couple to the reception and/or the hotel if there is no hired driver
- Oversees the transfer of gifts to a secure location after the reception
- Returns the groom's attire (if rented)
- Gives the groom moral support or assistance of any kind

DUTIES OF THE GROOMSMEN/USHERS:

- Arrive at the wedding location early to help with setup
- Assist in gathering the wedding party for photographs
- Attend to last-minute tasks such as lighting candles, tying bows on reserved rows of seating, etc.
- Roll out the aisle runner immediately before the processional
- Direct guests to the reception and hand out preprinted maps and directions to those who need them
- Collect discarded programs and articles from the pews after the ceremony
- Help decorate the newlyweds' car (optional)
- Escort guests to their seats as follows:
  - * Ask if they are guests of the bride or groom. The bride's guests should be seated at the left side of the church (facing the altar). The groom's guests should be seated to the right. (The reverse is true for Reform and Conservative Jewish weddings.)
  - * Seat the eldest guests first if a large group arrives.
  - * Escort female guests with the right arm as her escort follows, or lead a couple to their seat.

* Distribute programs to guests after they have been seated.
* Balance out the guests by asking arriving guests if they wouldn't mind sitting on the less-filled side.
* After the guests have been seated, escort special guests to their seats in this order (unless otherwise directed by the bridal couple):
  1. General special guests
  2. Grandmothers of the bride and groom
  3. Groom's mother
  4. Bride's mother

The Wedding Party Tracker

Keep all of your information organized and easy to find at a moment's notice with a roster of your wedding team.

Maid/Matron of Honor: _____
Phone/Cell phone: _____
E-mail: _____
Address: _____

Bridesmaid: _____
Phone/Cell phone: _____
E-mail: _____
Address: _____

Bridesmaid: _____
Phone/Cell phone: _____
E-mail: _____
Address: _____

Bridesmaid: _____
Phone/Cell phone: _____
E-mail: _____
Address: _____

Bridesmaid: _____
Phone/Cell phone: _____
E-mail: _____
Address: _____

Bridesmaid: _____
Phone/Cell phone: _____
E-mail: _____
Address: _____

Bridesmaid: _____
Phone/Cell phone: _____
E-mail: _____
Address: _____

Best Man: _____
Phone/Cell phone: _____
E-mail: _____
Address: _____

Groomsman/Usher: _____
Phone/Cell phone: _____
E-mail: _____
Address: _____

Groomsman/Usher: _____
Phone/Cell phone: _____
E-mail: _____
Address: _____

Groomsman/Usher: _____
Phone/Cell phone: _____
E-mail: _____
Address: _____

Groomsman/Usher: _____
Phone/Cell phone: _____
E-mail: _____
Address: _____

Groomsman/Usher: _____
Phone/Cell phone: _____
E-mail: _____
Address: _____

Groomsman/Usher: _____
Phone/Cell phone: _____
E-mail: _____
Address: _____

Flower Girl: _____
Parent's names: _____
Phone/Cell phone: _____
E-mail: _____
Address: _____

Ring Bearer: _____
Parent's names: _____
Phone/Cell phone: _____
E-mail: _____
Address: _____

Additional/Special Positions: _____
Phone/Cell phone: _____
E-mail: _____
Address: _____

Additional/Special Positions: _____
Phone/Cell phone: _____
E-mail: _____
Address: _____

Notes: _____
_____
_____
_____
_____

Parental Involvement

Just as you and your fiancé are excited about your wedding, your parents are feeling the same sense of excitement. The mother of the bride is almost always eager to help, but she is not the only family member who may want to participate in the wedding planning. Of course, the father of the bride has his moment in the spotlight, but you cannot forget about the soon-to-be in-laws. The relationship you share with these parties will affect your decision to include them or exclude them and to what extent.

The Mother of the Bride

Although you may not realize it, the mother of the bride is considered part of the wedding party. At the beginning of the ceremony, the seating of the bride's mother signals the ceremony is about to begin; she is the last person seated before the processional. As an official member of the wedding party, she does have official duties as well, including the following:

- Assists the bride in selecting her gown, accessories, and trousseau
- Helps the bride select bridesmaid's attire
- Coordinates her attire with the mother of the groom
- Work with the bride, groom, and groom's family to devise a seating plan
- Helps address invitations
- Helps attendants coordinate the bridal shower
- Assists the bride with wedding errands and activities
- Stands in the receiving line
- Acts as hostess of the reception

Parental Partnership

A wedding is the coming together of two families, and if your mother-in-law is itching to help, start off on the right foot and at least find a little something she can do. While you are at it, enlist the talents of your father-in-law and your father, too. Just remember, when and if you do decide to ask for assistance, do *not* ask for assistance in a category that you feel particularly passionate about and try to find tasks that are of some interest to the person. For example, if your in-laws are wine aficionados, ask them to lead the way in selecting wines for the cocktail hour and the meal.

Here are some jobs for these special people:

- Assist in locating wedding day transportation
- Prepare the family's guest list (have them "rank" guests in order of most necessary to invite to least necessary)
- Collect addresses and necessary information for invitations

- Research accommodations for out-of-towners (if they are local to the wedding venue)
- Sample cakes
- Mail wedding announcements on the day of the wedding
- Accompany you to the menu tasting
- Address invitations
- Select/Make/Assemble favors
- Get bride's gown and bouquet to preservationist after wedding
- Plan and host the rehearsal dinner (traditionally the groom's parents)

A Little Help from Your Friends

Most brides cannot justify or simply do not want twenty bridesmaids, but many feel that there is no other way to involve friends that they would like to be a part of their wedding. Well, no worries, there is much to be done, and delegating tasks will ease your workload while allowing others to contribute their talents and skills. Finally, don't forget there is another very important part of the wedding equation: the groom. The level of involvement from grooms is all over the board these days. Some grooms dive right in to the planning with the bride, and others prefer a laid back approach. Whatever the case, there are plenty of tasks he can help you with.

What They Can Do

Here are some ways to include friends and other special people in your wedding and wedding planning:

- Act as hostess/hostesses on the wedding day, directing guests to their seats, providing necessary information, and assisting with the guestbook and gifts
- Assist with addressing invitations and place cards
- Supervise the gift table at the reception, making sure that gift cards are secured to the gifts
- Make/assemble wedding favors and other small items
- Read at the wedding
- Act as a point person on the wedding day, ensuring vendors have arrived, the wedding party has their flowers, the reception is set up appropriately, etc.
- Play a musical selection or sing at the wedding or reception

"Friendly" Task Tracker

If you are going to be enlisting the assistance of your friends, you need to keep yourself organized and on track. Use the following space to keep on top of the tasks you have "assigned" and the progress that is being made.

Name:_____

Phone/Cell phone: _____

E-mail: _____

Date needed: _____

Task: _____

_____

_____

Name:_____

Phone/Cell phone: _____

E-mail: _____

Date needed: _____

Task: _____

_____

_____

Name:_____

Phone/Cell phone: _____

E-mail: _____

Date needed: _____

Task: _____

_____

_____

Name:_____

Phone/Cell phone: _____

E-mail: _____

Date needed: _____

Task: _____

_____

_____

CHAPTER 8

All Dressed Up

*Y*our walk down the aisle is one of the grandest moments of your life, and you should look and feel your best. The formality of the wedding will influence many of your decisions, but that does not mean you cannot inject some style and personality into your look. That being said, remember, it is not all about you. Your fiancé, the wedding party, and your parents are part of the wedding package, and also want to make a stylish statement.

The Bride's Ensemble

You may have dreamed about trying on wedding dresses since you were a little girl, but when you are looking for "the dress," you may actually feel a little overwhelmed. It is a lot of work to live up to your dreams. Working with a reputable bridal salon or seamstress will help make shopping for your gown enjoyable.

Shopping for the Dress

You should begin shopping for your gown as soon as you decide on the style and formality of your wedding and set the date. Ideally, you'll order your gown six to nine months before the wedding; some gowns can take that long to arrive from the manufacturer. You will also need to allot additional time for alterations. If you don't have a lot of time, some shops can turn an order in three months, but there may be rush charges, and you may not be able to have your first choice.

Begin by asking friends, family, coworkers, and your wedding planner for recommendations for a bridal salon. Check the pages of your phone directory, and visit a local wedding exposition. Once you find a place you're seriously interested in, ask for references, check with the Better Business Bureau (to verify that no complaints have been filed against the company), and look for reviews and comments online.

To receive the best possible service, always call the bridal salon and schedule an appointment. That will give you access to a knowledgeable bridal consultant who will assist you in finding the perfect gown, veil, and accessories. Be sure to take the following items: the proper undergarments, such as a strapless bra or bustier; shoes, in a heel height you typically wear; and any "must wear" jewelry or accessories. You may eventually replace some of these items, but you'll have a good idea of what works and what doesn't.

Shopping Tips and Hints

It's a good idea to take only one or two trusted people with you, usually your maid of honor (or bridesmaid) and your mother, so that you don't have too many opinions. However, there are no "rules" about who should accompany you; some brides have taken their grooms. Here are a few tips to make your experience more pleasurable:

- Always talk to the manager of the shop. Find out how long the place has been in business. (You would hope that a disreputable establishment would not be around long.)
- Be careful of counterfeit gowns. Some shops will tell you they carry brand-name merchandise, when the gowns are cheap imitations, sold to you at a "real" price. (Call the dress manufacturer or check online to verify that the shop is an authorized dealer for a particular designer.)
- Choose a delivery date that is several weeks before the wedding to give you time for alterations.
- Make sure that the bridal shop doesn't try to get you to order a size that is much too big or small for you. Don't expect the size of your wedding gown to be the same dress size you currently wear; bridal gowns are sized differently than ready to wear garments. Ask to see the manufacturer's size chart to see where your measurements fit in their sizing chart.
- Don't allow the shop to use cloth measuring tapes. Over time, the cloth begins to stretch, often yielding incorrect measurements.

- Ask for verification of your order; and call periodically to check on progress. (Sometimes the shops will hold your cash deposit for months before actually ordering your gown.)
- Get a written contract containing every aspect of your purchase agreement, including the delivery date, the cost of the dress, the cost of alterations, and any stipulations for refunds if the dress is not ready in time.

If you decide to have your dress made by a private seamstress, guard against the typical pitfalls. In addition, you may have to order your dress as much as a year in advance, because it can take that long to make a gown from scratch.

The Dress

The formality of your wedding is instrumental in achieving your vision. Traditional guidelines will get you started, but this is the twenty-first century and modern brides are forging their own path, and you can, too.

INFORMAL WEDDING:
- Formal, lacy suit or formal street-length gown
- Corsage or small bouquet
- No veil or train

SEMIFORMAL WEDDING:
- Chapel veil and modest bouquet (with floor-length gown)
- Shorter fingertip veil or wide-brimmed hat and small bouquet (with tea-length or midcalf-length gown)

FORMAL DAYTIME WEDDING:
- Traditional floor-length gown
- Fingertip veil or hat
- Chapel or sweep train
- Gloves
- Medium bouquet

FORMAL EVENING WEDDING (SAME AS FORMAL DAYTIME WITH THE FOLLOWING EXCEPTION):
- Longer veil

VERY FORMAL WEDDING:
- Traditional floor-length gown (usually pure white or off-white) with cathedral train or extended cathedral train
- Long sleeves or long arm-covering gloves
- Full-length veil
- Elaborate headpiece
- Cascade bouquet

Bridal Alternatives

If want an alternative, possibly less expensive route, the bridal salon's discontinued rack is not necessarily your sole option. The following alternatives to high-end retail have been known to pay off in major wedding day savings. Just remember, always check for quality: there should be no stains, rips, or other major flaws.

- **Heirloom or antique gowns.** Antique and heirloom gowns can be significantly less expensive than new ones (but they can also be pricey), and the added style and nostalgia they provide is priceless. Unless you're fairly petite, though, you may have a hard time finding one that will fit. Women and sizing specifications were a lot different many years ago. Some brides may also wish to wear their mother's wedding gown. If this interests you, consult a skilled seamstress to see if this is a possibility.
- **Used or consignment gowns.** Try consignment stores and other bargain outlets for previously worn gowns. These dresses can be bought for a fraction of the original retail cost and taken with you that day. Of course, finding a quality wedding gown on consignment may require some tenacity and detective work since they aren't readily available. If you're serious about taking the previously worn route, check out the classified section of the local paper and look on the Internet.
- **Outlet and warehouse sales.** Have you seen TV news coverage of a local warehouse's one-day wedding gown sale? Brides-to-be line up as early as 6 A.M. to get the first crack at wedding gowns, many boasting top designer names, marked down as low as $100 each. It sounds great, but watch out—bargain hunting can be a full-contact sport. In this maelstrom, women grab as many dresses as they can carry, irrespective of size, to increase the odds of finding a keeper. No one bothers much with dressing rooms either,

so if you're the modest type, be forewarned: women try dresses on right next to the rack. If the stress and the every-woman-for-herself atmosphere doesn't scare you off, you may very well walk away with a brand-new, top-quality gown.

- **Rent-a-gown.** Another increasingly popular way to find a gown is to rent one. Again, this option is not for someone who cares about being the first to wear the gown or who wants to keep it forever. Like a tuxedo rental, the gown is yours only for the wedding, then it's back on the rack for the next customer. Through rental, a famous-maker extravaganza that would cost thousands to purchase can be rented for only a few hundred. The major kink: if the gown you choose requires major alteration, they may not let you rent it. Think of how much valuable material would be lost in trying to fit a size twelve to a size four woman. After that, the dress could only be rented to very small women, a prospect the shop is unlikely to welcome.

- **A bridesmaid's dress.** An inexpensive alternative to a formal bridal gown is an elegant bridesmaid's dress in white (or even a color depending on your style). The dress can be embellished with some lace, buttons, and the like. It probably won't satisfy you for a formal wedding, but for a more informal event it can be a thrifty and inventive way to go.

The Finishing Touches

Your headpiece or veil should complement your gown, and there are plenty of options to explore. They are typically separate pieces, neither of which is mandatory, unless your house of worship requires a veil or some sort of head covering. There is also the option of jeweled hair pins, headbands, and faux or real florals to wear with your gown.

Although a headpiece or veil typically takes only eight to ten weeks to arrive after being ordered, consider placing your order even earlier. In this way, you can have a few trial runs with your hairdresser to ensure you'll get the look you want.

COMPLETING THE BRIDAL ENSEMBLE

- ❑ Slip
- ❑ Bra
- ❑ Hosiery
- ❑ Garter

- ❑ Gloves
- ❑ Shoes
- ❑ Jewelry (earrings, necklace, bracelet)
- ❑ Veil
- ❑ Headpiece (tiara, headband, hairpin, florals, etc.)
- ❑ Other

The Bridesmaids' Dress

Brides are famous for telling their bridesmaids, "Of course, you can wear it again." Although that may not be quite the truth, the days of ugly dresses are over. As any glance through a bridal magazine will show you, bridesmaids' dresses can be tasteful, elegant, and fashion-forward.

This is your wedding and should reflect your taste; therefore, you do not have to consult with the ladies about the bridesmaid's dress you select (they knew this when they accepted your invitation). You, can, of course, take their opinions into consideration, but they don't have the final approval.

Generally, the bridesmaids are dressed alike, but the dresses can differ in style. This makes it a lot easier to satisfy everyone; a dress that looks great on one woman can look like a potato sack on another. You can have the maid/matron of honor wear a different gown to help her stand out from the attendants. Try to keep the color, fabric, and hem length the same (or nearly the same depending on the case) to show some uniformity.

Keep the following suggestions in mind when shopping with your attendants:

- Check the formal dress section of a quality department store in your area before you go to a bridal salon. You may find appropriate dresses that your attendants can wear again—and at a better price than salon dresses.
- The attendants' dresses should complement your gown.
- Make sure the gown flatters all the ladies in the wedding party. It may be your wedding, but they are paying for this dress and if they feel good in their dresses, your photos will reflect it.
- Try to keep the cost within reason.
- If all of your attendants' shoes have to be dyed the same color, have them dyed together to ensure an exact color match.

Bridesmaid's Attire Checklist

The ladies of the wedding party have a lot to remember, so help them out and give them this list. Also, if, as a group, you will be getting your hair and makeup professionally styled, remind the bridesmaids to bring a button-front shirt. They can wear this shirt while their hair and makeup are being done and easily remove it to get into their dresses without messing up their hair or smudging their lipstick.

BRIDESMAID'S CHECKLIST

- ❑ Dress
- ❑ Shoes
- ❑ Pantyhose (two pairs)
- ❑ Proper undergarments
- ❑ Hair accessories
- ❑ Jewelry
- ❑ Handbag
- ❑ Makeup and hairstyling products
- ❑ Toiletries (including deodorant)
- ❑ Perfume

The Flower Girl

Flower girls are a sweet addition to a wedding. The flower girl's dress can match the attendants' dresses—or be completely different—but it should always be age appropriate. The flower girl may also wear white, accented or not with a color to match the wedding colors. The dress may be short or floor-length according to the style you want. If you have trouble finding something, a fancy party dress is a good and inexpensive choice.

Dressed to the Nines

The men, especially the groom (it is his day, too!), want to look their best on the wedding day as well. Typically, the groom and his attendants rent their formalwear and accessories. There are formalwear choices available to match the style demands of most weddings, and for the most part, all the men need to do is tell the store attendant what they're in the market for, and they're in business. On the other hand, they're not limited to rented formalwear. Depending on the locale and tone of your wedding, they can wear light-colored suits, thematic attire, or attire representative of your culture.

The Groom and His Men

The men should rent their formal wear one to three months before the wedding. Although a month is usually enough time to reserve the clothing in the "off season," it's better to be early during the peak wedding months (April–October). Obviously, the men should do business at a reputable shop that employs knowledgeable, helpful salespeople.

Formalwear Attire Guidelines

Here is a guide to help them dress the part.

INFORMAL WEDDING:

- Business suit (For the winter, consider dark colors; in the summer, navy, white, and lighter colors are appropriate.)
- White dress shirt and tie
- Black shoes and dark socks

SEMIFORMAL DAYTIME WEDDING:

- Dark formal suit jacket (in summer, select a lighter shade)
- Dark trousers
- White dress shirt
- Cummerbund or vest
- Four-in-hand or bow tie
- Black shoes and dark socks

SEMIFORMAL EVENING WEDDING:

- Formal suit or dinner jacket with matching trousers (preferably black)
- Cummerbund or vest
- Black bow tie
- White shirt
- Cufflinks and studs

FORMAL DAYTIME WEDDING:

- Cutaway or stroller jacket in gray or black
- Waistcoat (usually gray)
- Striped trousers
- White high-collared (wing-collared) shirt
- Striped tie
- Studs and cufflinks

FORMAL EVENING WEDDING:
- Black dinner jacket and trousers
- Black bow tie
- White tuxedo shirt
- Waistcoat
- Cummerbund or vest
- Cufflinks

VERY FORMAL DAYTIME WEDDING:
- Cutaway coat (black or gray)
- Wing-collared shirt
- Ascot
- Striped trousers
- Cufflinks
- Gloves

VERY FORMAL EVENING WEDDING:
- Black tailcoat
- Matching striped trousers trimmed with satin
- White bow tie
- White wing-collared shirt
- White waistcoat
- Patent leather shoes
- Studs and cufflinks
- Gloves

Men's Attire Checklist

Too many men dash into the formalwear shop and dash out without double-checking their order. Every male member of the wedding party should try on their tuxedos when they pick them up, making sure all the pieces of the tuxedo are there. Here's a list to give your men to ensure they remember to bring all the necessary items on the wedding day.

GROOMSMEN'S CHECKLIST
- ❏ Tuxedo/Suit (jacket, pant, shirt, suspenders, cufflinks, button covers, bow tie/tie, vest/cummerbund)
- ❏ Shoes

- ❏ White undershirt
- ❏ Dress socks in appropriate color (usually black)
- ❏ Toiletries (including deodorant)
- ❏ Cologne

The Little Guys

Most often the ring bearer and trainbearer are little boys, but they probably enjoy being dressed like the big guys. In most weddings, the ring bearer and trainbearers are dressed in the same basic outfit as the rest of the men (only in a much smaller size) or in a slight variation of the outfit featuring knickers or shorts

What about the Parents?

Of course you cannot forget about the parents. This is a big day for them too. It is a time for them to enjoy the fruits of their labors, and be proud of raising a fine son or daughter. Assist them with finding an appropriate outfit to wear that complements the other members of the wedding party as well as the wedding's formality.

The Mothers

Your mother, along with your fiancé's mother, will probably spend a great deal of time worrying about what to wear. After all, as hostesses, they want to look their best for their children's wedding. Work with your mothers to find dresses that will allow them each to look their best and to shine on your wedding day.

The mothers' dresses don't have to match, but they should be complementary in color, style, and length. Traditionally, your mother buys her gown first, in keeping with the style and colors of your wedding. She then consults your future mother-in-law, who should follow your mother's lead.

The Fathers

The style and color of the fathers' clothes should match that of the other male attendants. They can be differentiated with their accessories. For example, if the groomsmen are wearing vests instead of cummerbunds, the fathers can wear cummerbunds. Alternately, if the groomsmen are wearing colored accessories to match the bridesmaids, the fathers can opt for simple black accessories. If by some chance your dad already owns a tuxedo, and wants to wear it, have him pull it out and try it on. If it is acceptable to you, have it cleaned and pressed and purchase or rent the coordinating accessories.

CHAPTER 9

Showered with Gifts

A registry provides the bride with a trousseau, or the things that she and her husband will probably need during their first year of marriage. The word *trousseau* is a throwback to a time when brides brought their possessions with them into their new home. In time, the standard dowry eclipsed what one could carry in a small bundle, but the name stuck just the same. The days of dowries may be waning, but the need for a new bride to begin her marriage with a "hope chest" has not.

Home Sweet Home

When the time comes to register for your wedding, you and your fiancé should decide what items you need or would like to put on the registry. Many stores, as well as their online counterparts, offer complete lists and registry advice to aid in this process. Discuss colors, styles, and preferences for housewares and décor before finalizing your registry. Once you have some of these details in place, you can decide which stores are right for you to register at, and then officially establish your registries. This will enter you into the store's system and make your selections available for viewing by your guests.

Prepping for the Task

When making your wedding gift list . . .

❑ Shop with your groom so you make choices together
❑ Consider registering at two stores (at least) to give your guests a wider price range
❑ Discuss return policies with the bridal registrar
❑ Ask for a preprinted listing of gifts and household items the store offers
❑ List all pattern numbers and color choices
❑ Tell your family and friends where you're registered
❑ Suggest that gifts be sent to your home rather than brought to the reception
❑ Inquire with your insurance agent about coverage to protect the gifts while they're being displayed in your home

On a final note, some salespeople mistakenly tell you to put the stores registry cards in all of your invitations. Although it is acceptable to include this information with shower invitations, do not enclose these cards with engagement party or wedding invitations, as a gift is not a "requirement" for either of these events.

The Trousseau

The traditional bridal registry should include essentials for the home, but you do not need to register for anything you don't want or need. Although items such as formal china may seem ridiculous now, they may be useful in five or ten years when you have the family over for a holiday meal. Be sure to register for an adequate amount of items—for example, eight to twelve place settings each of china, silverware, and crystal, which would be enough to accommodate the guests at a dinner party or holiday meal.

Look at a sample registry. A vast selection of items in a wide variety of price ranges is ideal for a bridal registry.

FORMAL DINNERWARE:
(Specify manufacturer,
pattern, quantity)
❑ Dinner plates
❑ Sandwich/lunch plates
❑ Salad/dessert plates
❑ Bread and butter plates

❑ Cups and saucers
❑ Rimmed soup bowls
❑ Soup/cereal bowls
❑ Fruit bowls
❑ Open vegetable dishes
❑ Covered vegetable dishes
❑ Gravy boat

❏ Sugar bowl
❏ Creamer
❏ Small platter
❏ Medium platter
❏ Large platter
❏ Salt and pepper shakers
❏ Coffeepot
❏ Teapot
❏ Butter dish

**CASUAL DINNERWARE:
(Specify manufacturer,
pattern, and quantity)**
❏ Dinner plates
❏ Sandwich/lunch plates
❏ Salad/dessert plates
❏ Bread and butter plates
❏ Cups and saucers
❏ Rimmed soup bowls
❏ Soup/cereal bowls
❏ Fruit bowls
❏ Open vegetable dishes
❏ Covered vegetable dishes
❏ Gravy boat
❏ Sugar bowl
❏ Creamer
❏ Small platter
❏ Medium platter
❏ Large platter
❏ Salt and pepper shakers
❏ Coffeepot
❏ Mugs
❏ Butter dish

**FORMAL FLATWARE/SILVER-
WARE: (Specify manufacturer,
pattern, quantity)**
❏ Five-piece place setting
❏ Four-piece place setting
❏ Dinner forks

❏ Dinner knives
❏ Teaspoons
❏ Salad forks
❏ Soup spoons
❏ Butter spreader
❏ Butter knives
❏ Cold meat fork
❏ Sugar spoon
❏ Serving spoon
❏ Pierced spoon
❏ Gravy ladle
❏ Pie/cake server
❏ Hostess set
❏ Serving set
❏ Silver chest

**CASUAL FLATWARE: (Specify
manufacturer, pattern, quantity)**
❏ Five-piece setting
❏ Dinner forks
❏ Dinner knives
❏ Teaspoons
❏ Salad forks
❏ Soup spoons
❏ Hostess set
❏ Serve set
❏ Gravy ladle
❏ Cake/pie server

**GLASSWARE: (Specify
manufacturer, pattern,
quantity)**
❏ Wineglasses
❏ Champagne flutes
❏ Water goblets
❏ Cordials
❏ Brandy snifters
❏ Decanters
❏ Pitchers

BAR AND GLASSWARE:
(Specify manufacturer,
pattern, quantity)
- ❏ Beer mugs
- ❏ Pilsners
- ❏ Highball glasses
- ❏ Decanter
- ❏ Pitcher
- ❏ Cocktail shaker
- ❏ Ice bucket
- ❏ Champagne cooler
- ❏ Whiskey set
- ❏ Martini set
- ❏ Wine rack
- ❏ Bar utensils

HOLLOWWARE:
(Specify manufacturer,
pattern, quantity)
- ❏ Sugar/creamer
- ❏ Coffee service
- ❏ Serving tray
- ❏ Relish tray
- ❏ Canapé tray
- ❏ Chip and dip server
- ❏ Cheese board
- ❏ Cake plate
- ❏ Large salad bowl
- ❏ Salad bowl set
- ❏ Salad tongs
- ❏ Gravy boat
- ❏ Butter dish
- ❏ Salt and pepper shakers
- ❏ Round baker
- ❏ Rectangular baker
- ❏ Demitasse set

GIFTS/HOME DÉCOR ITEMS:
- ❏ Vase
- ❏ Bud vase
- ❏ Bowl
- ❏ Candlestick pair
- ❏ Picture frame
- ❏ Figurine
- ❏ Clock
- ❏ Lamp
- ❏ Framed art
- ❏ Brass accessories
- ❏ Picnic basket

SMALL ELECTRICAL
APPLIANCES:
- ❏ Coffeemaker
- ❏ Coffee grinder
- ❏ Espresso/cappuccino maker
- ❏ Food processor
- ❏ Mini processor
- ❏ Mini chopper
- ❏ Blender
- ❏ Hand mixer
- ❏ Stand mixer
- ❏ Bread baker
- ❏ Pasta machine
- ❏ Citrus juicer
- ❏ Juice extractor
- ❏ Toaster (specify 2-slice or 4-slice)
- ❏ Toaster oven
- ❏ Microwave
- ❏ Electric fry pan
- ❏ Electric wok
- ❏ Electric griddle
- ❏ Sandwich maker
- ❏ Waffle maker
- ❏ Hot tray
- ❏ Indoor grill
- ❏ Slow cooker
- ❏ Rice cooker
- ❏ Can opener
- ❏ Food slicer

- ❏ Electric knife
- ❏ Iron
- ❏ Vacuum cleaner
- ❏ Fan
- ❏ Humidifier
- ❏ Dehumidifier
- ❏ Space heater

CUTLERY:

- ❏ Carving set
- ❏ Cutlery set
- ❏ Knife set
- ❏ Knife block
- ❏ Steel sharpener
- ❏ Boning knife (specify size)
- ❏ Paring knife (specify size)
- ❏ Chef knife (specify size)
- ❏ Bread knife (specify size)
- ❏ Slicing knife (specify size)
- ❏ Carving fork
- ❏ Utility knife (specify size)
- ❏ Kitchen shears
- ❏ Cleaver

BAKEWARE:

- ❏ Cake pan
- ❏ Cookie sheet
- ❏ Bread pan
- ❏ Muffin tin
- ❏ Cooling rack
- ❏ Bundt pan
- ❏ Springform cake pan
- ❏ Pie plate
- ❏ Roasting pan
- ❏ Pizza pan
- ❏ Covered casserole
- ❏ Soufflé dish
- ❏ Rectangular baker
- ❏ Lasagna baker
- ❏ Lasagna pan

- ❏ Pizza pan
- ❏ Pizza stone

KITCHEN BASICS:

- ❏ Kitchen tool set
- ❏ Canister set
- ❏ Spice rack
- ❏ Cutting board
- ❏ Salad bowl set
- ❏ Salt and pepper mill
- ❏ Kitchen towels
- ❏ Potholders
- ❏ Apron
- ❏ Mixing bowl set
- ❏ Measuring cup set
- ❏ Rolling pin
- ❏ Cookie jar
- ❏ Tea kettle
- ❏ Coffee mugs

COOKWARE:

- ❏ Saucepan (small)
- ❏ Saucepan (medium)
- ❏ Saucepan (large)
- ❏ Sauté pan (small)
- ❏ Sauté pan (large)
- ❏ Frying pan (small)
- ❏ Frying pan (medium)
- ❏ Frying pan (large)
- ❏ Stockpot (small)
- ❏ Stockpot (large)
- ❏ Roasting pan
- ❏ Omelet pan (small)
- ❏ Omelet pan (large)
- ❏ Skillet
- ❏ Double boiler
- ❏ Steamer insert
- ❏ Wok
- ❏ Griddle
- ❏ Stir-fry pan

- ❏ Microwave cookware set
- ❏ Tea kettle
- ❏ Dutch oven

LUGGAGE:
- ❏ Duffel bag
- ❏ Beauty case
- ❏ Carry-on tote
- ❏ Pullman bags (specify quantity and sizes)
- ❏ Garment bag
- ❏ Luggage cart

HOME ELECTRONICS:
- ❏ Stereo
- ❏ CD player
- ❏ Television
- ❏ VCR
- ❏ Camcorder
- ❏ Telephone
- ❏ Answering machine
- ❏ Portable stereo
- ❏ Camera

FORMAL TABLE LINENS: (Specify color/theme):
- ❏ Tablecloth
- ❏ Place mats
- ❏ Napkins
- ❏ Napkin rings

CASUAL TABLE LINENS: (Specify color/theme):
- ❏ Tablecloth
- ❏ Place mats
- ❏ Napkins
- ❏ Napkin rings

MASTER BED: (Specify color/theme and bed size):
- ❏ Flat sheet
- ❏ Fitted sheet
- ❏ Pillowcase
- ❏ Set of sheets
- ❏ Comforter
- ❏ Comforter set
- ❏ Dust ruffle
- ❏ Pillow sham
- ❏ Window treatment
- ❏ Down comforter
- ❏ Duvet cover
- ❏ Bedspread
- ❏ Quilt
- ❏ Blanket
- ❏ Electric blanket
- ❏ Decorative pillows
- ❏ Down pillow (specify Standard, Queen, or King)
- ❏ Pillow (specify Standard, Queen, or King)
- ❏ Mattress pad

GUEST BED: (Specify color, theme and bed size):
- ❏ Flat sheet
- ❏ Fitted sheet
- ❏ Pillowcase
- ❏ Set of sheets
- ❏ Comforter
- ❏ Comforter set
- ❏ Dust ruffle
- ❏ Pillow sham
- ❏ Window treatment
- ❏ Down comforter
- ❏ Duvet cover
- ❏ Bedspread
- ❏ Quilt
- ❏ Blanket

- ❏ Electric blanket
- ❏ Decorative pillow
- ❏ Down pillow (specify Standard, Queen, or King)
- ❏ Pillow (specify Standard, Queen, or King)
- ❏ Mattress pad

MASTER BATH: (Specify colors)

- ❏ Bath towel
- ❏ Hand towel
- ❏ Washcloth
- ❏ Fingertip towel
- ❏ Body sheet
- ❏ Shower curtain
- ❏ Bath mat
- ❏ Bath rug
- ❏ Lid cover
- ❏ Hamper
- ❏ Scale
- ❏ Wastebasket

GUEST BATH: (Specify colors)

- ❏ Bath towel
- ❏ Hand towel
- ❏ Washcloth
- ❏ Fingertip towel
- ❏ Body sheet
- ❏ Shower curtain
- ❏ Bath mat
- ❏ Bath rug
- ❏ Lid cover
- ❏ Hamper
- ❏ Scale
- ❏ Waste basket

INTIMATES (for Bridal Shower)

- ❏ Peignoir set
- ❏ Short gown
- ❏ Long gown
- ❏ Camisole
- ❏ Tap pant
- ❏ Teddy

New Ways to Register

Sheets, napkins, and towels are important, but newlyweds cannot live by linen alone. Stores and websites, not normally associated with bridal registries, have jumped on board and now cater to a wide range of interests and needs. The following wedding gifts have been popular recently. Any of these items can be added to your bridal registry. Don't worry about the price tags; various guests can pitch in to buy you some of the more expensive items as a group gift.

Modern Options

These items are quickly becoming staples in the modern couple's registry. Consider these alternates if you have many of the items you need for establishing a home already.

NEW REGISTRY CHECKLIST

- ❏ Blue Ray disc player
- ❏ Camcorder
- ❏ Camping equipment
- ❏ Carpeting (gift certificate) or fine rugs
- ❏ CD-ROM drive for computer
- ❏ Closet storage/shelving
- ❏ Computer (laptop or desktop)
- ❏ Computer software
- ❏ Digital camera
- ❏ DVD player
- ❏ Garage door opener
- ❏ Gift card for favorite store
- ❏ Gift card for honeymoon excursion
- ❏ Microwave oven
- ❏ Portable DVD player
- ❏ Sewing machine
- ❏ Sporting equipment

More Possibilities

Couples and retailers are constantly finding new avenues for bridal registries. Consider the following options if you really have all you need for your home:

- **Honeymoon registry.** This service is offered, usually for a fee, by national travel companies, but it may also be offered by your local travel agent. Guests help you "purchase" the honeymoon by contributing. The service should provide a list of all contributors and their gifts to facilitate sending thank you notes.
- **Charitable registry.** If you really have everything you need, consider encouraging your guests to gift the charity of your choice instead. Various charitable organizations help you set up an online charitable registry that makes giving back easy.

CHAPTER 10

Party Time!

*D*on't forget about the other festivities that go hand-in-hand with a wedding celebration. Finally, after all the work you have been doing, there are a couple of celebrations that the bride does not have to plan—you just get to relax and let others take the reins. However, you'll still have to schedule some parties before and after the wedding to entertain your guests; it is a thoughtful and gracious gesture.

Showering the Bride

Once upon a time, it was customary to keep the specifics of the shower—time, date, location, and so on—a secret from the bride until the last moment. Times have changed, and now the maid of honor should consult the bride about the theme and the date. Unless the shower is a surprise, you need to compile a guest list (including addresses) and provide the names and locations of the stores where you're registered.

Planning the Shower

The typical bridal shower is held at a small hall or in someone's home, depending on the size of the guest list. Most bridal showers involve food and games. Traditionally the guests were women, but your fiancé is welcome. Co-ed showers are also growing in popularity, just try to avoid gender-specific activities and bridal shower games. Stick to a gender-neutral theme, as well.

Shower Menu Suggestions

The time of the day or evening will dictate the menu in almost all cases. The menu may also be inspired by the shower's theme or even the wedding's theme. Add the favorite dishes of the bride and groom as well. The following suggestions will help inspire your bridal shower cuisine.

BREAKFAST SHOWER:

- Bacon
- Bagels
- Belgian waffles
- Coffee cake
- Croissants
- French toast
- Fresh fruit
- Frittatas
- Ham
- Juices
- Mimosas
- Muffins or scones
- Omelets
- Pancakes
- Quiche
- Sausage

AFTERNOON SHOWER:

- Cold-cut platters
- Egg, tuna, or seafood salad
- Gourmet mixed-green salad
- Grilled vegetables
- Panini
- Pink champagne or punch
- Side salads (to complement the main dish), such as pasta, macaroni, or potato salad
- Sushi
- Tapas
- Tea sandwiches

HORS D'OEUVRES AND APPETIZERS:
- Cheese and crackers
- Beef teriyaki strips
- Bruschetta
- Chicken skewers
- Crab cakes
- Crudités (vegetable) platter with dip
- Fresh fruit with a dipping sauce
- Gourmet French fries
- Mini quiche, quesadilla, hamburger—almost any miniature version of a favorite food
- Scallops
- Shrimp cocktail
- Stuffed mushrooms
- Zucchini appetizers

DESSERTS:
- Brownies or Blondies
- Cake
- Chocolate fountain
- Chocolate-dipped strawberries
- Cupcakes
- Lemon squares
- Raspberry squares

Let the Games Begin

Games are a good way to get guests to interact and enjoy themselves, but they are by no means mandatory. The games should reflect the tone and theme of the shower. When the hostess is planning the shower, let her know how you feel about games and themes. Some bridal shower games are lighthearted but some are risqué. Here are some ideas for bridal shower games:

- **Guess the Goodies:** Fill a large decorative jar with white or colored candied almonds. Ask the guests to figure out how many almonds are in the jar. They can take as long as they want; at the end of the shower, ask them to hand in their answers on a slip of paper. The person who comes closest to the number wins the jar and the almonds. (Feel free to substitute another type of candy or perhaps the bride's or groom's favorite candy.)

- **Mish-Mash Marriage:** Scramble the letter in words associated with love and marriage: *kiss* (siks), *love* (voel), *garter* (tergar), and so on. Set a time limit for the guests to figure out the scrambles; the one who completes the most wins.

- **Mystery Spices:** Find ten jars filled with different spices. Place masking tape over the labels; spread the jars out on a table and let the guests try to guess what's in each jar. They may shake, examine, and even open and sniff the contents—just as long as they don't read the labels. Set a time limit and when it's up, the spices can go to the person who correctly guessed the identity of the most jars or to the bride to stock her kitchen.

- **Bride's Chatter:** Assign someone to keep a record of the bride's comments while she's opening her gifts. After she's through, read the comments back to the group. Taken out of context, the remarks are sometimes hilarious.

- **Famous Couple Trivia:** Develop some trivia questions with a love theme for your shower. Sample questions can be:
    * What pop princess, who got hitched on a whim in Las Vegas, had a marriage that lasted only 55 hours? (Answer: Brittney Spears)
    * What famous singing TV couple of the 1970s had their own show? (Hint: "I've Got You, Babe") (Answer: Sonny and Cher)
    * Dawson's Creek meets Top Gun . . . What famous couple married at a Castle in Italy? Bonus points: What was/is their tabloid nickname? (Answer: Tom Cruise and Katie Holmes, Tom-Kat)
    * Who were Lucy and Ricky Ricardo's best friends? (Answer: Fred and Ethel Mertz)

- **Memory Game:** After the bride-to-be has opened all of her gifts, ask her to leave the room for a few minutes. Pass out pencils and paper to the guests and ask them to answer questions about her: What is she wearing? What color are her shoes? Does she have nail polish on? Is she wearing earrings? What is her middle name? And any other questions you can think of. The guest with the most correct answers wins a prize.

- **Right Date Door Prize:** Ask all of the guests for the date of their wedding anniversary (or birthday for single guests). Whoever has a date that comes closest to the wedding date wins a prize.

- **Bride's Bingo:** This game can be bought at most stationery or card stores. The concept is the same as regular bingo; only words associated with weddings replace those boring numbers.
- **Pin It on the Groom:** If your live groom is unwilling to volunteer his services, draw the silhouette of a man on a large piece of paper. Attach a photo of the groom's face to the top. Blindfold the guests, spin them, and have them attempt to pin a flower on his lapel.

Handsome Rewards

If you anticipate resistance from a killjoy or two, here's the perfect incentive—prizes. Following are a few ideas with which you can reward the participants:

- Aromatherapy soaps
- Bubble bath/bath oils
- Candles
- Candy
- Coasters
- Coffee/tea mugs
- Gift cards for coffee
- Hand lotion
- Note cards or stationery

The Guest List

You don't have to invite all the women who'll be at the wedding to the shower. Usually, bridal showers are intimate get-togethers. You, your wedding attendants, family members, and five to thirty of your closest friends should make the party a success story. Multiple showers to accommodate different groups of friends, coworkers, and larges families are not uncommon. However, other than the wedding party and mothers (who are not obligated to bring a gift to more than one shower), guests should only be invited to one shower.

The Gift Recorder

The most important thing to remember is to assign someone the task of keeping track of your gifts. If you're in on the planning, bring this book with you and assign someone you trust with the task of filling out the following recorder. This way, you'll know who to thank for which gift.

✂ GIFT CHECKLIST

NAME	DESCRIPTION OF GIFT	THANK-YOU NOTE SENT?
1.		❏
2.		❏
3.		❏
4.		❏
5.		❏
6.		❏
7.		❏
8.		❏
9.		❏
10.		❏
11.		❏
12.		❏
13.		❏
14.		❏
15.		❏
16.		❏
17.		❏
18.		❏
19.		❏
20.		❏
21.		❏
22.		❏
23.		❏
24.		❏
25.		❏

Goodbye Single Life

Bachelor and bachelorette parties have a bad reputation, but there is no reason that you must follow *that* tradition. Think beyond the legends of drinking and carousing, and be more creative and adventurous . . . unless, of course, the traditional is what you had in mind.

Bachelor and Bachelorette Parties

Traditionally, sometime before the wedding, friends of the bride and groom take them out (separately, of course) to celebrate the end of their single days. These parties are not mandatory, but your single friends might be disappointed if you don't want one. While the bachelor party has been around for a long time, the bachelorette party only became popular in the latter half of the twentieth century, probably due to the sexual revolution, when women decided that going a little wild before the wedding was their "right," too.

The maid of honor, together with the other bridesmaids, is in charge of the bachelorette party, while the best man and groomsmen organize the bachelor party. The organizer may ask all attendees for contributions to pay for the shindig. Since party guests are not expected to bring gifts, it's perfectly all right, as long as all the invitees are told about the plans and financial arrangements in advance.

These parties were once held the night before the wedding, but now they're usually held a week or two before the ceremony, thus ensuring that the members of the wedding party will be fully recovered in time for the wedding.

Party Options

If a night on the town isn't right for you and your fiancé, there are options. Following are a few ideas. Remember, although the list may be divided into ladies' and men's categories, there is no reason there cannot be some crossover.

FOR THE LADIES:
- Spa day or weekend
- Wine tasting
- Comedy night
- Concert
- Play
- Crafting (such as painting pottery)

- Shopping and tea in the city
- Elegant dinner

FOR THE MEN:
- Pizza party
- Golfing (miniature or real)
- Sporting event (watching)
- Extreme sports (bungee jumping, BMX)
- Paintball
- Pool
- Poker
- Camping trip
- Casino

The Party Begins . . . The Party Continues

In addition to the excitement of the wedding itself, there are a few other wedding activities you may want to plan for your guests. These extra events are completely optional, and it is not your responsibility to plan out each minute of the guest's stay. However, if possible, the addition of parties before and after the wedding will surely be enjoyed and welcomed by the guests.

Before the Wedding

Many brides would like to invite the out-of-town guests and other special people to the rehearsal dinner, but space and budgetary limitations often preclude this option. To welcome those who have traveled so far (and some locals, too), try planning an informal gathering.

Ask a close friend or relative if they would be willing to host an informal get-acquainted cocktail party at their home, or plan to have everyone meet at the hotel, restaurant, or bar for a drink after the rehearsal dinner. Of course, plan this carefully because you should attend any events you invite guests to, at least for a while.

After the Wedding

Just because the reception is over, doesn't mean the parties are. With couples spending so much time carefully planning their weddings, and guests coming in from all over the country and even the world, brides and grooms have found new and fun ways to continue their wedding celebration as long as possible.

Post wedding parties include:

- **Brunches:** Day-after wedding brunches have become common and are customary in certain regions, but they are not mandatory. The agenda for the brunch is simple—eat, relax, and enjoy! The menu doesn't have to be extravagant either; a Continental breakfast with juices, coffee, and pastries will suffice. Extend this invitation to the out-of-town guests, and you may include locals as well.
- **Gift openings:** These gatherings may be "expected" in certain areas of the country. The newly married couple and their families gather together the day after the wedding and open their wedding gifts. The opening is usually at the bride's parent's home, and guests are welcome to attend. Light refreshment should be provided.

CHAPTER 11

Ready for My Close-Up

*W*hen the wedding is over, the glorious moments captured on film will help you remember the day and share the memories with future generations. Therefore, professionally documenting the important moments of your wedding day on film and video is essential for every wedding—and while preserving the memories is important, the bride and groom need to look their best, too. A little pampering will ensure these photos bring a smile to your face forever.

Your Best Shot

Your wedding photos will last a lifetime. When it is time to select the wedding photographer, do the research necessary to ensure you are getting what you want. If you understand the trends in wedding photography and the changes in technology, you will be on the right track to making an informed decision.

What You Need to Know about Photography

Deciding on the style you prefer and finding a professional photographer you like and with whom you work well are essential in capturing enduring images of your wedding. You should be familiar with some basic details that will influence the decisions you make.

As you review the following information about photography, keep in mind, there are a host of photographers who mix all of these approaches to create a unique style. The following information will acquaint you with the basics of photography basics:

- **Style.** Do you want a more photojournalistic approach, which documents the day as it unfolds, with less posing and more spontaneity? Do you prefer a more traditional style that includes more poses, utilizes lighting, and sets up shots? Or does an editorial approach, in which you seem to be posing for a magazine spread, appeal to you? Once you begin looking at photographers' sample books, your eye will guide you to the style you prefer.
- **Digital or film.** Although film was once highly preferred, high-end digital equipment can provide nearly the same quality. Some couples love the look of film, and some want the flexibility of digital. Each type of photography has pros and cons, so don't make a decision until you find the photographer you want. Many photographers shoot both formats.
- **Black and white or color.** Many couples feel that black-and-white photography has an artistic and timeless appeal. If you are shooting film, it is best to determine this in advance, as some quality may be lost when converting color prints to black and white. With digital, this is not a concern. Even if you love black and white, do not rule out having some color photographs taken. If you like the look of both, ask your photographer if she has the ability to shoot both color and black and white.
- **Personality.** An important aspect of wedding photography is the rapport you have with the photographer. You should like the photographer you hire. He doesn't need to become your new best friend, but his personality should be pleasing to you as well as the manner in which he presents himself. He will be with you much of the day, and he should be someone with whom you feel comfortable.

Making the Decision

Choose your photographer carefully; only sign on after you've seen his or her work and checked references. It's always wise to interview more than one photographer. That way, you can compare quality and prices to get the best person (and the best deal).

Questions to Ask

Here is a list of questions that will help you choose the best man, woman, or studio for the job.

❑ How long has the photographer been in this business?
❑ Does the photographer specialize in weddings? (If he or she isn't a wedding expert, find someone who is.)
❑ Is this a full-time photographer?
❑ Who is available/will be shooting the wedding (if the photographer is part of a larger studio)?
❑ Does the photographer shoot with a digital camera or with film? Or with both?
❑ Does the photographer shoot color only or is black and white or sepia available?
❑ Can you see samples of previous work and speak to some former clients?
❑ What is the photographer's style?
❑ Does the photographer have an assistant? Does the photographer have additional photographers who can be hired to shoot on the wedding day as well?
❑ Does the photographer offer an engagement session? At what cost?
❑ What types of photo packages are offered?
❑ What is included in the standard package?
❑ What are the costs for additional photos?
❑ How many pictures does the photographer typically take at a wedding of this size?
❑ In addition to the base package fee, will there be any additional hourly fees or travel costs?
❑ Will you be charged by the hour?
❑ Are there travel fees for shooting at more than one location, if the location is more than a certain amount of miles from the studio?
❑ Does the photographer keep the negatives? If so, for how long? If digital, is a disk of all the images available for purchase (or is it included)?
❑ Are negatives available for purchase?
❑ Will you be able to purchase extra photos in the future?
❑ Does the photographer use a variety of lighting techniques? A variety of backgrounds?

❑ Will the photographer take a mixture of formal and candid shots?

❑ Does the photographer shoot bridal portraits?

❑ Would the photographer be willing to incorporate your ideas into the shot list?

❑ Will the photographer provide a contract stipulating services, date, time, and costs?

❑ How long do we have to wait to see the proofs of our wedding photos?

❑ How long do we have to wait receive our albums and final prints of the wedding photos?

PHOTOGRAPHER WORKSHEET

Name of photographer/studio:

Address:

Telephone:

Contact:

Hours they can be reached:

Directions:

Appointments:

Time: Date:

Time: Date:

Time: Date:

Name of package (if applicable):

Date of hired services: Time:

Number of hours:

Overtime cost:

Travel fee:

Fee for custom pages:

Fee for black-and-white prints:

Fee for sepia prints:

Fee for album inscription:

Additional fees (if any):

Engagement session included?   _Yes   _No

Additional cost (if any):

Will attend rehearsal?   _Yes   _No

Additional cost (if any):

Cost of film, proofing, and processing included? _Yes _No

Additional cost, if any:

Type of wedding album included:

Date proofs will be ready:

Date final order will be ready:

Additional services included:

Cost:

Total amount due:

Amount of deposit: Date:

Balance due: Date:

Sales tax included?   _Yes   _No

Terms of cancellation:

Notes:

Included in package:

Number: Cost of each:

Notes:

Item:

Included:

Additional:

8″ × 10″ engagement portraits:

5″ × 7″ engagement prints:

4″ × 5″ engagement prints:

Wallet-size engagement prints:

Wedding proofs:

Wallet-size prints:

3″ × 5″ prints:

4″ × 6″ prints:

5″ × 7″ prints:

11″ × 14″ portraits:

Other prints (list):

Preview album: ....

Wedding album: ....

Wedding album pages: ....

Parent albums: ....

Other (list): ....

....

....

....

Click, Click, Click Goes the Shutter

Once you decide on a photographer, talk about the type and amount of photographs you'd like. Most professional wedding photographers know what photos they need to take and what photos a bride expects. But, the photographer won't be able to incorporate your ideas unless you communicate them. Create a list of the photographs you'll want the photographer to take on your wedding day. Here are some suggestions.

THE SHOT LIST

- ❏ Bride and groom
- ❏ Bride with her mother
- ❏ Bride with her father
- ❏ Bride with her mother and father
- ❏ Bride and groom with bride's mother and father
- ❏ Bride with siblings
- ❏ Bride with her mother and siblings
- ❏ Bride with her father and siblings
- ❏ Bride with her parents and siblings
- ❏ Bride with the grandparents
- ❏ Bride with the flower girl
- ❏ Bride with the ring bearer
- ❏ Bride and groom with the flower girl
- ❏ Bride and groom with the ring bearer
- ❏ Bride with the flower girl and the ring bearer
- ❏ The groom with his mother
- ❏ The groom with his father
- ❏ The groom with his mother and father
- ❏ The bride and groom with groom's mother and father
- ❏ Groom with siblings

- ❏ Groom with his mother and siblings
- ❏ Groom with his father and siblings
- ❏ Groom with his parents and siblings
- ❏ The groom with grandparents
- ❏ Bride and the groom with both sets of parents
- ❏ Groom with the flower girl
- ❏ Groom with the ring bearer
- ❏ Bride with her attendants
- ❏ Bride with each attendant
- ❏ The groom with his attendants
- ❏ The groom with each attendant
- ❏ The groom with bridesmaids
- ❏ The bride with groomsmen
- ❏ The entire wedding party
- ❏ Bride and groom with godparents and/or any favorite relatives

CANDID SHOTS BEFORE THE CEREMONY

- ❏ Bride in the final moments of getting ready
- ❏ Bride and her attendants at the bride's home/hotel before the ceremony
- ❏ Guests arriving
- ❏ Bride and her father arriving at the ceremony getting out of the car, and walking into the ceremony site
- ❏ Informal shots of bride and her attendants at the back of the church or ceremony site
- ❏ Informal shots of bride and her father before the ceremony
- ❏ Signing of the Ketubah or other cultural rituals (if necessary)

TRADITIONAL CEREMONY SHOTS

- ❏ Each attendant walking down the aisle, including the flower girl, the ring bearer, and pages
- ❏ Bride's mother coming down the aisle
- ❏ Groom's parents coming down the aisle
- ❏ Bride and her father coming down the aisle
- ❏ Bride's father leaving bride at the altar
- ❏ Wedding party at the altar
- ❏ Bride and groom exchanging vows and rings
- ❏ The lighting of candles and any other special ceremony features
- ❏ Bride and the groom kissing at the altar
- ❏ Bride and groom getting into the car

❏ Bride and groom toasting each other in the car
❏ Bride and groom leaving the ceremony
❏ Group shot of guests at end of ceremony or at the beginning of the reception (if possible)

RECEPTION
❏ Bride and groom's grand entrance
❏ First dance
❏ Father/daughter dance
❏ Mother/son dance
❏ Cake cutting
❏ Best man's toast
❏ Bride and groom toast
❏ Tossing the garter
❏ Tossing the bouquet
❏ Table shots
❏ Bride and groom leaving the reception
❏ The "getaway" car

DECORATIVE ELEMENTS
❏ Ceremony setup
❏ Details of ceremony (programs, bouquets, etc.)
❏ Reception tables
❏ Place settings
❏ Overall reception room setup
❏ Details of the reception
❏ Cake (prior to cutting)
❏ Other special requests: _____
_____
_____
_____
_____

More Photography Needs

In addition to the traditional wedding photographs, you may want some of following areas covered:

- **Engagement portrait:** Most wedding photographers offer engagement sessions when you book their services either as part of the package or at a reasonable rate. The engagement session is a great time to connect with your photographer and get a feel for how he works. This is also a time for the photographer to get a feel for the chemistry between you and your fiancé and to see how you photograph together. These photos may be printed along with your engagement announcement in the newspaper and/or displayed at the bridal shower, and other parties.

- **Wedding announcements:** If you're planning to send a wedding announcement to the newspaper, be sure to inform your photographer so she can take an appropriate photo to meet each publication's requirement (check with each publication for the specifics).

- **Bridal portrait:** The bridal portrait is an optional tradition that is not as common today. Some brides have a formal bridal portrait taken for cultural reasons. These portraits are not taken on the wedding day, but rather in advance and are usually formal posed studio shots.

Caught on Film

For many couples, live-action footage of their wedding is equally as important as the photographic images. How else are the bride and groom going to see and hear everything they were too excited or dazed to be aware of while it was actually happening? As with still photography, be very careful about whom you trust with the responsibility of capturing your wedding memories as they unfold.

Videography Know-How

The special moments of your wedding cannot be duplicated, so it's usually not a wise idea to hire a family member or friend to be your videographer. They may do adequate work, but they probably still can't provide you with the same quality you'd get from a professional. (They probably won't have the necessary editing equipment, for one thing.).

With all of the equipment and technology available today, look for a broadcast-quality wedding movie. Get the best deal for your money, but pay a little more for the person who will do a wonderful job. Although it is still called videography, almost all professionals supply the bride and groom with DVDs.

Name That Format

Although there are a variety of videography styles, not all videographers are skilled in shooting all of them. Here are some options that are pretty standard for weddings. The difference in style is due primarily to the skill of the videographer and his or her editing techniques. Ultimately the style you decide on will be determined by your budget and the skill level of the professional you hire.

- **The Basic Package.** This format uses one camera; thus, it is the least expensive option. No editing is required, but the videographer can still add small touches, such as names and dates. This is a great option if your budget is tight, but you still want to capture your ceremony and a few special events.
- **The Documentary.** This format gives you a documentary-style account of your wedding day. It begins with getting dressed and then proceeds to the ceremony and the reception, sometimes adding interviews with family and friends. The price varies widely depending on the type of equipment used and the amount of editing needed.
- **The Love Story.** This option usually starts with photographs of you and your groom as children or young adults. From there, it shows you sharing your lives. The ceremony, reception, and shots of your honeymoon (sometimes) end this format. It can be quite expensive because it takes a little more work to put together.

Questions to Ask

When interviewing videographers, the same advice applies as when you selected a photographer. For the most part, ask the same types of questions and apply the same scrutiny. Your videographer will be interacting with you and your guests throughout the wedding, so his or her personality and rapport with you and your groom is very important. Here are some things you'll want to ask.

- ❑ How long has he been doing this professionally?
- ❑ Are samples of her work available? Will she give you references?
- ❑ Is the work guaranteed?
- ❑ Can you look at a work-in-progress in addition to a demo DVD? (This way you'll know that the videographer is actually doing the work, not buying a great demo DVD from someone else.)

❑ Is the equipment high-quality, including the editing and dubbing machines?

❑ How many cameras will be used? How big will the staff be?

❑ What special effects are available?

❑ Will you use wireless microphones during the ceremony?

❑ How is the fee computed? Flat rate? Hourly?

❑ Is a standard package deal offered? Is so, what is it?

❑ How much will it cost to have copies of the original made?

❑ Is the raw (unedited) footage available for purchase?

WHEN VIEWING SAMPLE DVDS, CONSIDER THE FOLLOWING QUESTIONS:

❑ Do the segments tell a story, giving a clear sense of the order in which the events took place?

❑ Does the DVD capture the most important moments, such as cutting the cake and throwing the garter?

❑ Is there steady use of the camera, clear sound, vibrant color, and a sharp picture?

❑ How are the shots framed? What editing techniques are used?

❑ Does the tape move smoothly from one scene to the next, rather than lurching ahead unexpectedly?

On a final note, be sure to ask your videographer about any technological advances in cameras or editing that might be available. Because technology develops so quickly, equipment may be available now that was unheard of even six months ago.

❧ VIDEOGRAPHER WORKSHEET

Name of videographer/studio:

Address:

Telephone:

Contact:

Hours they can be reached:

Directions:

Appointments:

Date: Time:

Date: Time:

Date: Time:

Name of package (if applicable):

Date of hired services: .... Time: ....
Number of hours: .... Number of cameras: ....
Overtime cost: ....
Travel fee: ....
Additional fees (if any): ....
Will attend rehearsal? .... _Yes _No ....
Additional cost, if any: ....
Length of videotape: ....
Date tape will be ready: ....
Videotape will include: ....
Prewedding preparations: .... _Yes _No ....
Notes: ....

Individual interviews with bride and groom prior to
ceremony: .... _Yes _No ....
Notes: ....

Ceremony: .... _Yes _No ....
Notes: ....
Reception: .... _Yes _No ....
Notes: ....
Photo montage: .... _Yes _No ....
Notes: ....
Other: ....

Package includes: ....
....

Sound: .... _Yes _No ....
Notes: ....
Music: .... _Yes _No ....
Notes: ....
Unedited version of wedding events: _Yes _No ....
Notes: ....
Edited version of wedding events: _Yes _No ....
Notes: ....
Price of additional copies of videotape: ....
Other: ....

Additional services included:

Cost:

Total amount due:

Amount of deposit: Date:

Balance due: Date:

Sales tax included?   _Yes   _No

Terms of cancellation:

Notes:

Bridal Beauty and "Groom"ing

Of course you want to look your best on your wedding day—and your groom does, too! Prepare yourself and your sweetie by devising a complete regimen of hair, skin, and health care as soon as you start your planning. Some simple dos and don'ts will help you develop your beauty calendar.

- Never get a "new" haircut or change your hairstyle right before your wedding. Not only do you run the risk of "looking like a stranger in your own hair," but you might wind up hating your new coif and feeling miserable on your big day.
- Getting a facial on the day of your wedding, or anytime close to it, is also ill-advised. Most professional facials involve rigorous cleansing methods that can leave skin looking blotchy, reddened, or even damaged for a few days to a week afterward. If you want a facial, schedule it at least a week or two in advance.
- Do not use tanning the day of or the day before the wedding.
- Wax facial hair in advance; this harsh treatment may cause temporary irritation and blotchiness on your otherwise radiant visage.

Facials, waxes, artificial tans, and drastic haircuts aside, there is no proper or improper way to pamper yourself on your wedding day. If you feel confident in your ability to style your own hair, apply your own cosmetics and do your own nails, there's no need to make a trip to the salon. Of course, if you're anything at all like the majority of brides, you'll reach for the security of professional stylists come wedding day.

Hair, Beautiful Hair!

As a bride, you have choices. Of course, you can do your hair yourself, or you can hire someone to do it for you—live it up, you are the bride! Depending on who you select to do your hair on the wedding day, you may have to go to the stylist's salon, or you can find a stylist to come to the comfort and convenience of your home/hotel. Whatever option you choose, pay attention to some basic hair dos:

- Make an appointment to consult with your hairdresser or hired stylist a few months before.
- Schedule a trial run. Bring your headpiece and ask the stylist to try a few options.
- Ask the hairdresser if he/she can come to you. How much extra would this cost? Do you have to pay more for work that runs overtime, and how much?
- Make sure the hairdresser knows exactly where and when to meet you.
- Wear a button-down shirt when getting your hair styled. There's nothing worse than realizing you're going to have to cut yourself out of your favorite shirt, or ruin your hair pulling your shirt over your head.

Put on a Happy Face

Like your hairdresser, a professional makeup artist can help you feel more confident or give you a completely new look. Even if you're already satisfied with your daily makeup selection and application skills, you may want to try something different for your wedding day. A professional makeup artist will ensure you have that wedding day glow without looking overly made up or overdone. It is important that you look and feel comfortable in your own skin. Ultimately, you want to look a little more glamorous. Here are some makeup dos:

- Schedule a consultation with a trusted makeup artist in your price range.
- Go in for a practice session (trial run), just so there are no surprises on the day.
- If you like the makeup application, make an appointment for the day of your wedding.
- Ask if the makeup artist can come to you? If yes, how much would this service cost?

Nails

Even if you've always considered manicures to be frivolous, you might want to make an exception for your wedding day. Well-manicured nails and beautiful hands are another part of the complete bridal beauty package. If your regular routine includes caring for your nails, and that is your preferred look, then you shouldn't need any special attention—just make an appointment with your emery board! However, if you are interested in a little something extra, here are some options for beautifying your hands:

- A French manicure accents the white half moons at the tips of your fingernails and gives them a high buff. This option costs a little more but is well worth the time and expense.
- Acrylics provide real-looking nails. If you're a biter, this is the way to go.
- A standard manicure shapes and polishes the nails.
- As for colors, stick with subtle shades such as sheer pink or off-white. Stay away from the fire-engine reds and the offbeat bright or super-dark shades; these colors might be fun for the honeymoon, but they would probably raise eyebrows during the ceremony.

CHAPTER 12

I Now Pronounce You . . .

*P*lanning your wedding ceremony too often takes a backseat to the "fun" part of planning. After all, it is much easier to debate colors of purple and select table linens than to get in touch with your feelings and think about the seriousness of the commitment you are about to make. So what happens . . . the ceremony plans, other than the date, are put on the back burner . . . until now. Some simple steps will show you how easy it can be to plan your ceremony, from obtaining the license to walking down the aisle.

Walking Down the Aisle

When you selected your ceremony location (see Chapter 6), you probably decided on the style of ceremony you will have as well as who may be officiating. These decisions are the building blocks for planning your ceremony and will jump-start other stylistic and logistic choices you will need to make for your ceremony.

Ceremony Preparation

If you have decided on a religious ceremony, consult with your officiant about premarital requirements. Religions vary in their rules and restrictions, as do different branches within the same religion. Your first meeting with the officiant should clear up most of the technical details and give you the opportunity to ask questions. Although religions differ too much to make a blanket statement about each one's approach to the marriage rite, the following should give you a general idea about what to expect from some of the major religions' ceremonies.

Catholic Ceremony

Contrary to popular belief, the Catholic ceremony is not overly long. You have the option of incorporating a complete mass (which adds about fifteen minutes to the total time), but it is not a requirement. From the moment the organ announces your arrival at the altar to the time you walk back down the aisle with your new husband, approximately half an hour will have elapsed. Here are the basic elements of the ceremony:

- **Introductory Rites:** The ceremony starts with opening music selections; once you reach the altar, the priest greets you and your guests, offers the penitential rites, and says an opening prayer.
- **Liturgy of the Word:** This is when the reading you have chosen will be given, perhaps by special friends or family members. At the completion of the reading, the priest gives a brief homily that focuses on some aspect of marriage.
- **Rite of Marriage:** After the declaration of consent, the rings are blessed and exchanged. What most people don't realize is that the exchange of vows, not the ring exchange, is the act that marks the official moment of marriage.

The Protestant Ceremony and Preparations

Protestant marriages of all denominations have far fewer requirements and restrictions than Catholic marriages. An informational meeting with the clergy is required, but premarital counseling is optional. Furthermore, there is no need for an annulment if either party has been divorced.

The Protestant religion encompasses a great many denominations, but the basic elements of the marriage ceremony are the same. Here's a brief overview of what to expect:

- The ceremony begins; members of the wedding party walk up the aisle.
- The couple welcomes their guests.
- A Prayer of Blessing is said.

- Scripture passages are read.
- There is a Giving in Marriage (affirmation by the parents).
- The congregation gives its response.
- Vows and rings are exchanged.
- The celebration of the Lord's Supper takes place.
- The unity candle is lit.
- The Benediction is given.
- The Recessional takes place.

Jewish Ceremonies and Preparations

Judaism, too, has different branches that adhere to different rules; however, in the Orthodox, Conservative, and Reform traditions, certain elements of the wedding ceremony are basically the same.

- The marriage ceremony is conducted under a chuppah, an ornamented canopy (optional in the Reform ceremony).
- The Seven Blessings are recited.
- The bride and groom drink blessed wine; the groom then smashes the glass with his foot (the glass is wrapped in a napkin to prevent shards from landing in someone's eye or from harming the groom's foot).
- The newly married couple is toasted with the expression "Mazel tov!" ("Good luck!").

Jewish marriages within the more stringent Orthodox and Conservative branches have a few stipulations:

- Weddings cannot take place on the Sabbath or any time that is considered holy.
- Ceremonies are performed in Hebrew or Aramaic only.
- No interfaith marriages are conducted.
- Men must wear yarmulkes.
- The bride wears her wedding ring on her right hand.

While Reform ceremonies also cannot take place on the Sabbath or any other holy time, they do differ from Orthodox and Conservative ceremonies in a few ways. For example, the bride wears her ring on her left hand, and in English-speaking countries, the ceremony is performed in both English and Hebrew.

Interfaith Marriage

Early in the planning, consult with both sets of clergy to get a clear picture of what rules and restrictions each religion, clergy, and house of worship has. Some clergy will accept the union, and others will with stipulations. For example, some will allow co-officiating, and some will have restrictions about where or when the marriage takes place. Here are a few ground rules for interfaith marriages. Again, always check with your clergy for specifics.

- In general, the Catholic Church will sanction a marriage between a Catholic and non-Catholic providing that all of the church's concerns are met.
- In marriages between a Protestant and a Catholic, officiants from both religions may take part in the ceremony if the couple wishes, and arrangements are made in advance.
- Quakers, Hindus, and Buddhists, to name a few, are more open and accepting of interfaith marriages.
- The Church of Latter-Day Saints, Reform Judaism, and Islam will tolerate these unions.
- For-hire officiants representing all denominations perform ceremonies all over the country. They are usually more flexible in their rules and guidelines. Now you may not be able to marry in a house of worship, but you just might be able to have officiants from both faiths perform the ceremony at a neutral or agreed-upon location.

Questions to Ask the Officiant

Armed with the knowledge of the types of ceremonies and the rituals associated with them, it is time to finalize some details with your officiant. When you meet with your ceremony officiant to discuss a wedding date, have a list of questions ready. Find out what you will be required to do. Here is a list of potential questions:

- ❏ Are there any restrictions placed on your ability to marry?
- ❏ What is the procedure for an interfaith marriage?
- ❏ Are there any papers to be filled out or bans to be posted?
- ❏ Are there any premarital counseling requirements? If so, what are they?
- ❏ What does the ceremony consist of?

❑ May we write our vows?
❑ What kind of services does the facility provide (music, reception area)?
❑ What fees are required for marrying in the facility? What are the costs?
❑ What do the fees include?
❑ Is it possible to include family members and close friends in the ceremony as readers, candle lighters, singers, and such?
❑ Are there any restrictions on the kind of music?
❑ What are the rules regarding photography and video recording?
❑ Will there be a coordinator for the ceremony site, or does the officiant handle those details?
❑ Are there facilities for the bridal party to wait in while they wait for the ceremony to begin?

✄ **CEREMONY CHECKLIST**

Ceremony site: _____

Address: _____

Officiant name: _____

Phone number: _____

Additional meetings/premarital counseling sessions:

Place: _____ Date: _____ Time: _____

"I Do! I Do!"

Once you have determined the venue, who will be marrying you, and whether it will be religious or civil, it is time to plan the ceremony. Even if you have been to hundreds of weddings, you probably have not paid a lot of attention to what happens and when. As an observer, your job is easy, but now it is your turn to walk down the aisle. Suddenly, everything means something, and everything has a time and place.

Ceremony Outline

Each ceremony will differ slightly, but there is a basic guideline for traditional parts of a wedding. Depending on your officiant and type of ceremony, there are many ways to customize the guidelines with readings, musical selections, and symbolic ceremonies.

THE WEDDING CEREMONY:

- **Prelude.** The thirty minutes or so prior to the ceremony as guests arrive and are seated.
- **Processional.** Signals the beginning of the ceremony. The mothers are seated, followed by the entrance of the officiant, groom, and groomsmen. The bridesmaids, followed by the ring bearer and flower girl are next, and of course the bride and her escort are the grand finale.
- **Welcome.** The officiant welcomes the guests.
- **Giving Away or Recognition of the Parents.** The officiant asks some version of "who gives this woman to marry this man?"
- **Charge to the Couple.** The officiant confirms each party has come to marry of his or her free will.
- **Exchange of Vows.** The couple recites their vows.
- **Ring Ceremony.** The bride and groom each give and receive a wedding ring symbolizing their union.
- **Pronouncement.** You are officially married.
- **Recessional.** The official exit from the church as a married couple. You and your husband will lead the recessional, followed by pairs of the bridal party in the reverse order in which they entered. The parents are also included.

The Vows

If you're perfectly satisfied with the traditional civil or religious vows, skip to the next section—individualized vows aren't for everyone. However, if you're looking for something different to say at the altar, an alternative to the traditional wedding vows, this list of questions is designed to help you find the perfect vows for you and your fiancé.

Start by writing down answers to the following questions. Doing so will provide you with valuable source material, and help you develop your vows.

Answer together: How do you, as a couple, define the following terms?

Love: _____

_____

_____

Trust: _____
_____
_____

Marriage: _____
_____
_____

Family: _____
_____
_____

Commitment: _____
_____
_____

Togetherness: _____
_____
_____

Answer together: How did the two of you first meet?
_____
_____
_____

Answer separately: What was the first thing you noticed about your partner?

Bride: _____
_____
_____

Goom: _____
_____
_____

Answer together: List any shared hobbies or other mutual interests.
_____
_____
_____

Answer together: What was the single, most important event in your relationship? (Or, what was the event that you feel says the most about your development as a couple?)

_____
_____
_____

Answer together: How similar (or different) were your respective childhoods? Try to recount some of the important parallels or differences.

_____
_____
_____

Answer together: Is there a song, poem, or book that is particularly meaningful in your relationship? If so, identify it here.

_____
_____
_____

Answer together: Do you and your partner share a common religious tradition? If so, identify it here.

_____
_____
_____

Answer together: If you share a common religious tradition, is there a particular scriptural passage that as a couple you find particularly meaningful? If so, identify it here.

_____
_____
_____

Answer together: Why did your parents' marriages succeed or fail? What marital pitfalls do you want to avoid? What can you take from your parents' examples, good or bad?

_____
_____
_____

Answer together: Take some time to reminisce about the course of your relationship. When did you first realize you loved each other? When did you first say the words? What trials and tribulations has your love had to overcome? What are your fondest memories?

_____
_____
_____

Answer separately: What do you love about your partner? Why?

Bride: _____
_____
_____

Goom: _____
_____
_____

Answer together: How do you and your partner look at personal growth and change? What aspects of your life together are likely to change over the coming years? How do you anticipate dealing with those changes? How important is mutual respect and tolerance in your relationship? When one of you feels that a particular need is being overlooked, what is the best way to address this problem with the other person?

_____
_____
_____
_____

Answer together: Do you and your partner have a common vision of what your life as older people will be like? Will it include children or grandchildren? Take this opportunity to put into words the vision you and your partner share of what it will be like to grow old together.

_____
_____
_____
_____

First Draft of Our Wedding Vows

_____

_____

_____

_____

_____

_____

_____

_____

_____

_____

_____

_____

_____

_____

_____

_____

_____

_____

_____

_____

_____

Second Draft of Our Wedding Vows

_____

_____

_____

_____

_____

_____

_____

_____

_____

_____

_____

_____

_____

_____

_____

_____

_____

_____

_____

_____

_____

The Wedding License

What do driving, fishing, hunting, boating, selling alcohol, and getting married have in common? Legally, you need a license for every
one of them. Admittedly, you're not threatening the public safety by
getting married (unless you're planning a particularly festive reception), but that license binds you as a couple in the eyes of the law.

The Marriage License

The criteria required to get a marriage license vary from state
to state. Contact your local marriage bureau (usually at the city or
county clerk's office) to find out exactly what you'll need to do. If you
are marrying in another county or state, check into the laws and regulations in that area. Marriages performed in another jurisdiction are
typically considered legal if the requirements for marriage were met
where the marriage occurred.

You and your groom must apply together for a marriage license.
Beyond that, requirements vary from state to state and county to
county, and may change at any time. Be prepared to provide, produce, or prove any or all of the following requirements:

✄ MARRIAGE LICENSE CHECKLIST
....

- ❏ Birth certificate
- ❏ Driver's license
- ❏ Proof of age or consent of parent, guardian, or judge if under
  eighteen
- ❏ Proof of citizenship
- ❏ If required, completed blood tests and doctor's certificates
- ❏ Proof of death, divorce, or annulment (in the case of a previous
  marriage)
- ❏ Pay a fee. A check, cash or money order is typically acceptable
  payment (credit cards are not always accepted).

Get Me to the Church on Time

How you arrive at and depart from your wedding ceremony and reception is your choice. Although limousines are still the most popular mode of wedding transportation, don't overlook the possibility of dropping down to the ceremony in a hot-air balloon, floating up on a sailboat, or trotting in on a stallion. There are dozens of options. Of course, whatever means of transportation you choose should fit into your budget.

Here are some ideas:

- A trolley car
- A horse and buggy (or just a horse)
- A sleigh
- A plane
- A glider
- An antique car
- A classic car
- An Excalibur, a Rolls-Royce, a Bentley, or another make of luxury car
- A parade float
- A motorcycle
- A unicycle (well, maybe not—it might be tough to maneuver in the gown)
- A speedboat
- . . . anything else you can think of!

Granted, some of these options aren't practical year-round, and others can be a logistical nightmare—not every ceremony site comes equipped with a landing strip—but you have choices beyond the traditional limousine.

Finally, if you're not renting transportation, but borrowing a nice luxury car from a family member or friend, make sure the car is tuned up, cleaned, and filled with gas. (Offer to pay for the car wash and fill the tank with gas before and after the wedding.)

Questions to Ask

To ensure that you'll be getting quality transportation for your money, ask the following questions. (Note: the following list is geared toward limousine rental, but it will give you an idea of the kind of information you should get from any transportation supplier.)

- ❑ How long has the company been in business?
- ❑ Does the company have the proper license and insurance?
- ❑ Can you get references from former customers?
- ❑ Does the company own its vehicles? (Companies that don't own their vehicles may have a hard time guaranteeing availability. They are also less likely to be on top of any mechanical problems or other unforeseen dilemmas.)
- ❑ Can you inspect the vehicles? (Check for cleanliness, dents, rust, and so on.)
- ❑ Does the company have the kind of vehicle you want? The color you prefer? Will it be available on your wedding day?
- ❑ What are the rates? (Most limousine services charge by the hour. Unfortunately, the clock starts ticking the minute they leave their home base rather than when you start using the vehicle.)
- ❑ What is the company's cancellation policy?
- ❑ Is there a required minimum fee or number of rental hours?
- ❑ What is the policy on tipping? Is it included in the hourly rate, or should you account for it separately? (You won't want to tip your chauffeur at the end of the night if the gratuity is covered in the fee you paid. It's doubtful the service will be so spectacular that you'll want to pay twice.)
- ❑ How much of a deposit is required to reserve the vehicle(s) for your wedding? When is the final payment due?
- ❑ Will the company provide champagne? Ice? Glasses? A television? Will these items cost extra?

🌿 TRANSPORTATION CHECKLIST

Company name: _____
Phone: _____
Contact person: _____
Phone: _____
Type and color of vehicle: _____
Number of people the vehicle holds: _____
Rental includes: _____
_____
_____

Rate (overtime also): _____

Cancellation policy: _____

Deposit required: _____

Balance due: _____

May We Hitch a Ride?

You are also responsible for providing or arranging transportation for the members of your wedding party. You might also want to make sure your parents and the groom's parents won't be standing on the corner waiting for a bus to the ceremony. If your budget allows, consider renting an extra limousine or two to chauffeur them to and from the ceremony and reception sites. Otherwise arrange for those with the nicest cars to transport the rest of the group. Make sure everyone is aware of who's taking whom, what time people will have to be ready, and where they may have to meet.

The Going-Away Car

If you're lucky, your budget will allow you to keep your limousine (or other rented transportation) until the end of the reception. As your attendants may not be too keen on trashing a rented luxury car, you can whip over to your hotel (or to the airport) in style and not have to worry about cans clanging behind you all the way.

Before it's too late, be aware of the tradition of "decorating" the going-away car. Usually the male attendants are responsible for this. For safety's sake, make sure they don't obstruct the view or movement of the driver. Any writing should be applied with washable shoe polish.

CHAPTER 13

The Party of Your Life

*M*any brides feel pressured to have a large, formal reception because they think their guests expect it or, more often than not, because they think that is how it is supposed to be. Truth is, the guests just want to celebrate with you, and a reception can be just about anything you want. Deciding between an informal cocktail hour or a plated meal is only part of the story; there is more to the reception than just the meal.

The Perfect Party

The wedding reception is most likely the biggest, most expensive party you will ever plan. It is the ultimate celebration of this glorious event in your life. After the many, many months you have been planning and looking forward to this day, it is time to relax and enjoy with your family and friends.

What Happens When

A wedding reception has three basic parts: the cocktail hour, meal service, and dancing. Here are brief explanations of each part:

- The cocktail hour lasts for approximately one hour (sometimes a little less, sometimes a little more). It allows the couple and wedding party to finish their photos and freshen up before the grand entrance. Now, if you feel uncomfortable calling this time a cocktail hour—because of the time of day or even due to religious considerations—simply call it a gathering time.

- At the conclusion of the cocktail hour, the guests are escorted to the dining area for the meal. Once they find their seats, the first order of business is the grand entrance. Then the wedding meal is served. Traditional elements continue throughout the meal and remainder of the evening.
- Once the meal is complete, dancing begins and the party really starts. More than likely, there will be formal protocol dancing and then the guests will be invited to join in. The cake is cut, and the bouquet and garter are tossed.

Traditions

There are many ways to structure the flow of events at a wedding reception. It depends on what you want to do and what kind of reception you want to have. You can work with your wedding planner, location manager, and musical entertainment to personalize or develop your itinerary. Use the following list to determine which traditions you want to include in your reception timeline.

Keep in mind, what all these traditions mean and what they are for, as you prepare the reception timeline in Chapter 14. At that time, you will be formulating the specific details of these events as well as selecting appropriate musical selections to accompany them.

RECEPTION TRADITIONS AND EVENTS CHECKLIST

❏ **Grand entrance.** The grand entrance is the first introduction of the bride and groom at the reception. This is generally the first order of business once the guests are in their seats, as everyone's attention is focused. Traditionally the bride and groom, as well as the entire wedding party, are formally announced into the reception, but recently, couples are making a change and introducing only the bride and groom.

❏ **Welcome by the bride's father.** This is an optional activity. If you choose to include it, the father of the bride (or host of the wedding) usually greets and welcomes the guests soon after the guests take their seats, prior to the best man's toast.

❏ **Toast by the best man.** The best man traditionally makes the first toast to the bride and groom. His toast should take place toward the beginning of the evening, either prior to the meal service or at some point early in the meal service.

❏ **Bride and groom greet the guests.** This is a popular option in lieu of having a receiving line. During the meal service, the bride and groom go from table to table to greet the guests and thank them for coming.

❏ **First dance.** Traditionally, no one should take the dance floor until the bride and groom have their first dance. There are many opportunities to do the first dance earlier in the reception so if your guests are feeling the music and want to get up and dance the floor will be open.

❏ **Father/daughter and/or mother/son dance.** The father/daughter dance can be held after the first course is served or once the meal concludes. The groom and his mother may join in during this dance or dance to their own song.

❏ **Wedding party dance.** Each attendant dances with the partner he or she walked down the aisle with or dance with a spouse or significant other.

❏ **Cake cutting.** The bride and groom cut the first piece of cake together. A small slice of cake is placed on a plate, and then the groom feeds the bride a small bite, followed by the bride doing the same to the groom. Cake is then served to the guests.

❏ **Bride and groom toast/thank-you speech.** At some point during the reception, the groom toasts the bride, the bride toasts the groom, or the couple thanks the guests for coming.

❏ **Garter and bouquet toss.** The long-standing tradition of these events is that whoever catches the bouquet or garter will be the next to marry. The single men/ladies at the reception usually gather in a particular area so the bride/groom can (blindly) toss the garter/bouquet. If you are planning to include the toss, ask the florist to make you a toss bouquet, which are usually included at little to no charge.

❏ **Send off or getaway.** This is the formal exit of the newlyweds and the conclusion of the event. Either the couple can stay for a last dance and then make their way to the getaway car or a more complicated exit can be orchestrated utilizing bubbles, sparklers, and so on.

Please Be Seated

Imagine a flurry of hungry wedding guests entering the reception not knowing where to go, where to sit, what to do. Worse yet, picture your grandmother scrambling for a table only to be seated with your hard-partying college roommates or next to the band's speaker. Now, doesn't that make you realize the importance of a proper seating plan?

The Head Table

The head table is wherever the bride and groom sit and is the focus of the reception. It usually faces the other tables, near the dance floor. The table is sometimes elevated, and decorations or flowers are usually low enough to allow guests a perfect view of the bride and groom.

Traditionally, the bride and groom, honor attendants, bridesmaids, and groomsmen sit at the same table. While you can always adopt the "rules are made to broken" mentality, tradition dictates that parents, spouses, or children of attendants, and child attendants do not sit at the head table. The bride and groom sit in the middle and everyone clusters around them.

Rather than hosting a traditional head table, many couples are opting for a sweetheart table, which is a table just for two . . . you and your new husband. Many couples prefer this option as it lets them have a little time together to eat their meal. The wedding party would sit at one or two guest tables designated for them, and often are able to sit with their spouses or significant others for the meal service.

The Seating Plan

A seating plan falls just short of being considered a necessity, but it is a courtesy and convenience for your guests. Guests, especially those who don't know many people, often feel uncomfortable without assigned seating. If you're planning a cocktail party, or not planning to serve a full meal, a seating plan isn't necessary, but you should have enough tables and chairs to accommodate all of your guests.

HERE'S HOW TO FORMULATE A SUCCESSFUL SEATING PLAN:

- Get a floor plan from the venue. It should outline the layout of the room (dance floor, bar, guest book, gift table, etc.).
- You need to decide where you will be sitting, as well as where the other tables of honor with the wedding party and your families will be positioned.
- Ask how many guests may be seated at each table. A general rule is eight to ten guests at a sixty-inch round table. This will determine the number of tables you will need for dining.

- Decide if you are going to solicit input from your families when determining who should sit where.
- Begin matching guests by families, where you know them from, or by similar interests. From here, you will be mixing and matching until you have the right guests at the "right" seats.
- Place people in the room to best accommodate their special needs. Chances are Grandma doesn't want to sit by the band's speaker and the kid's table shouldn't be next to the head table. Think also about wheelchair accessibility.

Places, Please

Now that the importance of the seating plan is clear, you need to decide how to let guests know where they are seated. The easiest way to indicate the guests' table assignments is to have escort cards (folded tent cards with the guest's name and table number printed on them) situated near the reception room entrance. Guests pick up the escort card to find their table assignment. If you are only assigning guests to a table, they may then find any seat they wish at that table. If you would like to designate a place setting, you will also need place cards on the table.

Thank You for Coming

Your guests have traveled from near and far to be a part of your wedding celebration. It is only polite and hospitable to acknowledge this and thank them for their presence and well wishes. Greeting the guests at the ceremony or reception with a receiving line and providing the guest with a small token in the form of a favor are two simple ways to show your appreciation.

The Receiving Line

Many couples are not quite sure what a receiving line entails or what to do in one. They can only envision a long line of guests waiting . . . and waiting. So, it's usually the first thing to get axed. However with proper protocol and a plan, the receiving line can be a lot of fun for you and a great way to connect with the guests.

Traditionally, the receiving line should form after the ceremony but before the reception. You can have it at either site. Just keep in mind that the receiving line is only as time-consuming as you make it. Here's who may participate (in order, beginning at the head of the line):

- Bride's mother
- Bride's father (optional)
- Groom's mother
- Groom's father (optional)
- Bride
- Groom
- Maid of honor
- Best man (optional)
- Bride's attendants

Traditionally, participation by the father and the best man in the receiving is optional. If you do choose to include them, their proper positions are outlined in the preceding list.

If you skip the receiving line, you must greet your guests and make them feel welcome. Provided it doesn't interfere with serving the meal, go from table to table to greet the guests throughout the event. Continue between courses, during the meal, and if necessary, as the dancing begins. Your parents may also want to visit the tables.

Favors

Saying thank you to the guests by way of a wedding favor is a tradition that has survived the test of time. Your guests will take these small tokens of appreciation as they leave your wedding. Favors can be as simple or elaborate as you'd like, depending upon your budget. If you're having a theme wedding, it's nice to have a memento to correspond with your theme.

FAVOR IDEAS

- ❏ A seedling for a tree to plant at home
- ❏ Candles
- ❏ Candy-coated almonds
- ❏ Candy, the bride and groom's favorite selections
- ❏ A charitable donation, made in lieu of individual favors
- ❏ Chocolate, gourmet boxed
- ❏ A locale- or destination-inspired item
- ❏ Packets of seeds
- ❏ Picture frames
- ❏ Soaps
- ❏ Wine or champagne

CHAPTER 14

Entertain Us!

*M*usic creates atmosphere and sets the tone for your wedding. You will want to plan out your musical genres according to the activities taking place. The musical selections for the ceremony are thoughtful and joyful, while the tempo picks up for the cocktail hour and then reaches its peak during the reception. A mix of music is often necessary to make your younger and older guests happy. By selecting varied styles of music, everyone will find something to keep them entertained.

"Here Comes the Bride"

Before you begin to pick out music for your wedding ceremony, keep in mind that in a house of worship, the music will need to be religious in tone. Check with the officiant for current guidelines; policies on the appropriate selections in a religious setting do evolve. Find out what you can use before you get your heart set on something. On the other hand, if your wedding is not being held in a house of worship, almost anything goes.

You should also be sure to:

❏ Meet with the musical director from your house of worship to discuss appropriate selections

❏ Discuss fees for the organist and any additional musicians that may be provided

❏ Choose the selections for each distinct part of the ceremony at least two months before the wedding

The Prelude

The prelude music sets the mood and provides listening enjoyment for your guests as they await your arrival. It should begin twenty to thirty minutes before the ceremony starts and end as the mothers and grandmothers are preparing to be escorted down the aisle.

The Processional

After the mothers are seated, the processional is played as the wedding party makes its way down the aisle. When the bride begins her walk, something selected especially for her is played. (An alternative, however, is for the bride to walk down the aisle to the same tune as the rest of the party, played at a different tempo.)

SOME PROCESSIONAL FAVORITES INCLUDE:
- "Waltz of the Flowers," Tchaikovsky
- "Wedding March," Mendelssohn
- "The Bridal Chorus" ("Here Comes the Bride"), Wagner
- "Trumpet Voluntary," Dupuis
- "Trumpet Voluntary," Clarke
- "Trumpet Tune," Purcell
- "The Dance of the Sugar Plum Fairies," Tchaikovsky
- "Ode to Joy," Beethoven
- "The March," Tchaikovsky
- "Ave Maria," Schubert
- "The Austrian Wedding March," traditional

The Ceremony

During the ceremony, you may wish to hear songs that have a special meaning. It is very nice to have a piece of music played while the couple is participating in symbolic rituals where there is no speaking, such as the lighting of the unity candle, the wine ceremony, or taking communion. If nothing comes to mind, ask your officiant for ideas. He or she will probably be able to suggest dozens of wonderful songs that can add meaning to the event.

SOME CEREMONY FAVORITES INCLUDE:
- "My Tribute," Crouch
- "The Lord's Prayer," Malotte

- "Panis Angelicus," Franck
- "Now Thank We All Our God," Bach
- "Saviour Like a Shepherd Lead Us," Bradbury
- "Cherish the Treasure," Mohr
- "We've Only Just Begun," The Carpenters
- "The Unity Candle Song," Sullivan and Haan
- "The Bride's Prayer," Good
- "The Wedding Prayer," Dunlap
- "All I Ask of You," Norbet and Callahan
- "Wherever You Go," Callahan
- "The Wedding Song," Stookey
- "The Irish Wedding Song," traditional

The Recessional

The recessional is played at the conclusion of the ceremony, as the members of the wedding party make their way back down the aisle. This music should be joyous and upbeat to reflect the new happiness in your life. Many couples are making a break from the traditional and playing modern musical selections that really reflect their personalities. Of course, if you are in a house of worship, be sure to check if you can play modern tunes for the recessional.

SOME RECESSIONAL FAVORITES INCLUDE:
- "The Russian Dance," Tchaikovsky
- "Trumpet Tune," Stanley
- "Toccata Symphony V," Widor
- "All Creatures of Our God and King," Williams
- "Trumpet Fanfare (Rondeau)," Mouret
- "Pomp and Circumstance," Elgar
- "Praise, My Soul, the King of Heaven," Goss

Cocktails, Anyone?

The cocktail hour is when the wedding party and families finish with the photography and the guests arrive at the reception location. During this time, refreshments and light fare should be served, and it is a nice touch to provide some entertainment.

Entertainment Options

The entertainment can be as simple or as elaborate as suits your event. Some options include:

- Use prerecorded music from the venue's sound system
- Use an iPod or mp3 player
- Ask the DJ if he can provide a small sound system for cocktail area
- Ask the band if a couple of the musicians are available to play (and then join the band later)
- Hire live musicians, anything from a strolling guitarist to a mini orchestra
- Hire magicians, fortune tellers, or tarot card readers

Let's Dance

Most reception entertainment consists of a live band or a disc jockey and should be reserved about eight months in advance of the wedding. The music at your reception is a key element in its success. Select appropriate music that appeals to all ages for a truly successful musical plan. Additionally, include music and dances from your family's ethnic heritage to liven up your reception.

Before interviewing musical entertainment, discuss the following items with your location manager. It would be heartbreaking for you to shell out thousands of dollars on a band to discover that your venue is located in a residential area and amplified music is not allowed, or that your rural locale has no power. Additionally, visit the site with your band or DJ before making any formal commitment. Consider these questions:

- ❏ Can the reception site accommodate your band or DJ?
- ❏ Is there enough electrical power? Outlets? Space?
- ❏ How are the acoustics?
- ❏ Are there restrictions on amplified sound or a noise curfew at the venue?

Live Versus Recorded

You will hear many arguments about why a disc jockey is better than a band or visa versa. Ultimately it comes down to your preference for prerecorded music versus live music. Bands look impressive up on the stage and have traditionally been considered to be more formal. However, bands are considerably more expensive, and many couples want to hear their musical selections as they know them, not as a band plays them, so either choice has become perfectly acceptable at a formal wedding. The DJ or bandleader also typically acts as the emcee for the event.

When you are selecting the musical entertainment, you do not have to settle for a loud band or a cheesy DJ that will spoil the mood. Professionals will tailor their repertoire to your needs. Tell the group what you want, and if they cannot do it, look elsewhere. Consider hiring a combination of musicians, such as a strolling violinist for the cocktail hour and throughout dinner, and a DJ for the dancing portion of the evening.

CONSIDER THE FOLLOWING WHEN HIRING A BAND:

- Do you like the group's sound? (Is it appropriate for your wedding?)
- How good is the band's sound system?
- Is their overall appearance and demeanor positive? (Do band members look happy about what they're doing?)
- Do they have a wide repertoire of material? (Do they balance various styles well? Is there a good mix of fast and slow songs?)
- Would you trust the band leader to serve as master of ceremonies if need be? (Will he or she charge extra for this?)

CONSIDER THE FOLLOWING WHEN HIRING A DISC JOCKEY:

- Is the equipment and sound system of good quality?
- Does he have a large musical library?
- Does she mix different sounds and styles well? Is there a good mix of fast and slow songs?
- Would you trust him to serve as master of ceremonies, if need be? (Is there any additional fee?)

Questions to Ask

As with every wedding vendor you hire, interview the musicians carefully and ask for references. Use the following questions when interviewing potential entertainers.

❏ What is the band's specialty/forte?
❏ Does the band specialize in rock and roll, jazz, blues, etc.? Does the DJ specialize in a certain style or sound or genre of music?
❏ How many members are in the band? Does the DJ work alone or have an assistant?
❏ What is your attire for the event?
❏ What equipment do you bring? Do you have a song list that we have to use? Are you willing to learn/find special requests?
❏ What are the fees? How many hours does that include? Is overtime available? At what cost?
❏ How many breaks do you require during a typical four- or five-hour reception? How do you accommodate our musical needs during your breaks?
❏ What are the costs?
❏ Are there any fees not included in the quote?
❏ Is a special sound system or hookup required?
❏ What is the cancellation policy?
❏ What are the payment terms? (Ask about deposit and balance amounts.)

It's a Deal

Some details should never be left to chance, so make sure to get the following stipulations in writing.

- The attire. You don't want to see anyone wearing ripped jeans and gym shorts to a wedding, much less to *your* formal wedding.
- The arrival time. Make sure that the band or DJ has enough lead time to set up gear before the guests arrive. This is especially important for bands; sound checks don't often make for soothing dinner music.
- The exact cost of the services and everything that price includes. Some bands charge you if they have to add an extra piece of equipment; some DJs charge for special requests. Find out in advance about everything you'll be expected to pay for.
- The band or DJ's knowledge of the exact location of the reception. Sounds elementary? Well, believe it or not, there have actually been instances where the musical talent has shown up at the right hotel, but in the wrong city!

RECEPTION MUSIC WORKSHEET

Name of band/DJ:

Address:

Telephone:

Manager/contact:

Hours he or she can be reached:

Number of performers:

Description of act:

Demo tape available?   _Yes   _No

Notes:

View live performances?   _Yes   _No

Date: Time: Location:

Appointments:

Date: Time:

Date: Time:

Date: Time:

Date of hired services: Time:

Number of hours:

Cocktail hour:

Overtime cost:

Includes the following services:

Equipment provided:

Equipment rented:

Rental costs:

Cost:

Total amount due:

Amount of deposit:

Date:

Balance due:

Date:

Terms of cancellation:

Notes:

Reception Music Checklist

When you hire professional musical entertainment, you do not need to direct the musical selections for every moment of the reception. The talent should be able to read the crowd's mood and judge what music would be appropriate based on prior discussions with you. You may want to select special pieces of music for certain events.

Here is a checklist of events that your master of ceremonies (i.e., band leader, disc jockey, or other) and reception site coordinator will discuss with you in regard to the reception. Complete this form to determine the happenings at your reception and include your preferred musical selection for the events. Once you do this, your reception will take shape quickly.

Introduce entire bridal party? ❑ Yes ❑ No
Music: _____
Introduce only bride and groom? ❑ Yes ❑ No
Music: _____
Parent(s) of bride: _____
Parent (s) of groom: _____
Grandparent(s) of bride: _____
Grandparent(s) of groom: _____
Flower girl(s): _____
Ring bearer(s): _____
Bridesmaids: _____
_____
_____
Groomsmen/Ushers: _____
_____
_____
Maid/Matron of honor: _____
Best man: _____
Bride and groom as they are to be introduced:
_____
Receiving line at reception? ❑ Yes ❑ No   When _____
Music: _____
Blessing? ❑ Yes ❑ No   By whom: _____
First toast? ❑ Yes ❑ No   By whom: _____
Other toasts? ❑ Yes ❑ No

By whom: _____
_____
_____

First dance: ❑ Yes ❑ No   When _____
Music: _____
To join in first dance: _____
_____

Maid of honor and best man? ❑ Yes ❑ No
Parents of bride and groom? ❑ Yes ❑ No
Bridesmaids and ushers? ❑ Yes ❑ No
Guests? ❑ Yes ❑ No
Father/daughter dance? ❑ Yes ❑ No
Music: _____
Mother/son dance? ❑ Yes ❑ No
Music: _____
Wedding party dance ❑ Yes ❑ No
Music: _____
Open dance floor for guests after first dance? ❑ Yes ❑ No
Cake cutting? ❑ Yes ❑ No
Music: _____
Bouquet toss? ❑ Yes ❑ No
Music: _____
Garter toss? ❑ Yes ❑ No
Music: _____
Last dance? ❑ Yes ❑ No
Music: _____
Other event: _____
When: _____
Music: _____
Other event: _____
When: _____
Music: _____
Other event: _____
When: _____
Music: _____

CHAPTER 15

Flowers, Décor, and a Whole Lot More

ridal magazines depict glorious weddings with lavish décor and stylish themes—the stuff of dreams. This is what brides love to look at and talk about. Beautiful florals, dramatic lighting, and unique rentals enhance the look of your wedding and set it apart from the others. When it's time to dress up your wedding venue, find inspiration in these fabulous creations and think about all the aspects that create a truly fabulous setting for your one-of-a-kind day!

Flower Power

Everyone expects to see flowers at weddings, and why not? They are beautiful to look at and lovely to smell. No matter how grand or how simple, flowers have a great impact on the visual presentation of your wedding. When used creatively, they are an effective means to enhance the environment.

The Florist

When you meet with professional floral designers, they should listen to your concerns and wishes. Bring fabric swatches and tear sheets from magazines to convey the look you are trying to achieve. They can also offer advice on the types of florals that fit your budget and season and give you their perspective on trends and colors. When you hire a florist, you should receive a detailed contract and proposal highlighting the number of flowers you need, as well as the types, colors, and pricing, and setup and delivery schedules.

Questions to Ask

After you have researched found a couple of florists you want to interview, make an appointment to discuss your needs. Use this list of questions to assist you in your selection process.

- ❏ What is your specialty or style?
- ❏ Do you have arrangements that will fit my budget?
- ❏ Do you have a portfolio of previous weddings and events we can review?
- ❏ May I have a list of references?
- ❏ Can you match or complement the color scheme of my wedding? (Bring your color swatches.)
- ❏ Will you visit the ceremony and reception venue to get a feel for what type of flower décor is needed?
- ❏ How many weddings do you handle on a given day/weekend?
- ❏ If we reuse flowers from the church at the reception, can you help transport the arrangements?
- ❏ What is the cutoff date for making changes to our order?
- ❏ Is there a delivery fee?
- ❏ What is the cancellation policy?

Floral Checklist

Who needs flowers? Where and what type of flowers do you need? These are simple questions to answer if you use the following checklist.

🌸 FLOWERS FOR THE WOMEN

The Bride
Bridal bouquet
Toss bouquet (optional)
Floral headdress/flowers for hair
Going-away corsage
Other: _____
_____

To be delivered to: _____
Time: _____
Cost: _____

Bridal Attendants
Matron/Maid of honor
Bridesmaids
Flower girl basket
Floral headdresses/flowers for hair (optional)
Other: _____
_____

To be delivered to: _____
Time: _____
Cost: _____

❧ FLOWERS FOR THE MEN

Groom's boutonniere
Best man's boutonniere
Groomsmen's boutonniere
Ring bearer's boutonniere
Other: _____
_____

To be delivered to: _____
Time: _____
Cost: _____

❧ FLOWERS FOR THE FAMILY AND HONORED GUESTS

Bride's mother
Bride's father
Groom's mother
Groom's father
Stepmother(s)
Stepfather(s)
Grandmothers
Grandfathers
Mothers' roses
Aunts, cousins, special friends, godparents
Other: _____
_____

To be delivered to: _____
Time: _____
Cost: _____

❧ FLOWERS FOR WEDDING HELPERS AND PARTICIPANTS

Officiant
Soloist
Readers
Instrumentalist
Guest book attendant
Gift attendant
Hostess
Other: _____
_____
To be delivered to: _____
Time: _____
Cost: _____

Ceremony Site
Aisles
Aisle runner
Altar floral spray
Arch/Canopy
Candelabra
Petals for aisle
Pews
Other: _____
_____
To be delivered to: _____
Time: _____
Cost: _____

Reception Site
Bar
Cake (if desired)
Cake table
Centerpieces for tables
Cocktail tables
Drapes, garlands, or greenery
Flower petals for tossing
Gift table
Head Table
Miscellaneous tables (place card, gift, and guestbook)

Plants, trees, shrubs
Restrooms
Sweetheart table
To be delivered to: _____
Time: _____
Cost: _____

Rehearsal Dinner
Centerpieces
To be delivered to: _____
Date: _____
Time: _____
Cost: _____
The Florist
Company: _____
Contact: _____
Phone: _____
Address: _____
Deposit made: _____
Final payment due: _____
Last day for changes: _____

Mood Lighting

Lighting has been a popular addition to high-end events for some time. It has now become increasingly popular for weddings of all budgets. The lighting need not be extravagant, even simple touches can make a huge impact on the look and feel of your wedding.

Types of Lighting

Event lighting is very different than the standard lighting at a venue. Event lighting includes everything from washing the walls with color to spotlighting guests' tables to your monogram floating around the dance floor. For these lighting services, you will need the services of a professional lighting designer. Also, be sure to talk to your venue/venues about restrictions and lighting capabilities before you go forth with these plans.

Some typical lighting choices include:

- **Uplighting.** Light that is projected onto a wall or (vertical) surface. The lights are placed low, usually on the ground and shine up. Color acetate sheets, called gels, can be placed over the lights to create different colors.
- **Pin spots.** Focused beams of light used to highlight or accent a particular item, such as the cake or the centerpiece at each table.
- **Gobos.** A metal template with a design cut into it that is placed over theatrical or event lighting to produce a pattern on the wall or floor.
- **Spotlight.** A focused beam of light that draws attention to a particular aspect of the reception such as the entertainment.

If professional event lighting is out of your budget, consider the following:

- Candles add a warm feel, enhance the atmosphere of most room, and are a great addition to almost any décor. Always check with your venue because many cities have strict fire codes.
- Use the venue's lighting system by asking the event manager or your wedding planner to raise and lower the venue's lights at appropriate moments. For example, they can raise the lights during dinner so guests can see, but bring them back down during dancing—nothing can kill the dancing more than a room of bright lights.
- Twinkle lights can easily be strung around many railways and trees. Just be sure to okay it with the venue, allow yourself enough time to do it, and remember the extension cords.

On a final note, depending on your venue, consider utilitarian lighting. Many unique and outdoor venues available to couples do not have the necessary built-in lighting to allow the guests, caterers, and vendors to see properly. You may find yourself in need of lighting services just to pull off the event.

LIGHTING CHECKLIST
Some areas you may want to highlight with event lighting include:

- ❑ Altar/Arch/Location of vows
- ❑ Cake table

❑ Dance floor
❑ Entrance to the venue/venues
❑ First dance, spotlight
❑ Landscape (paths, perimeter of a lawn, a terrace)
❑ Reception/Guest tables
❑ Walls (color wash with uplighting)

Borrowed Style

Beyond basic party rentals, which you may or may not need depending on your venue, are a huge variety of fun extras that make your décor pop! You can have sofas, coffee tables, tents, even movie props—for a price.

Necessities

Most hotels, country clubs, and established wedding venues have all the basics you need, such as china, glassware, staging, and lighting. Most likely, you will only need to worry about rentals if you want something more than what they are offering. Ask the site manager if they work with other rental companies that can supply these items. You will often be able to upgrade certain items, such as chairs and linens, sometimes at a lower cost through the venue.

Most major rental companies have knowledgeable representatives to help you. Look for a company that will offer this more personal service. If you are trying to outfit your entire event with rentals, and don't have a wedding planner, you may be able to ask your caterer for assistance and advice.

QUESTIONS TO ASK
❑ What are the delivery charges? How and when does overtime begin?
❑ What are regular delivery hours?
❑ Are you familiar with the site?
❑ When are the rentals dropped off? Picked up?
❑ How are the rentals priced?
❑ When do you need a final count for the items?
❑ Is a deposit required?
❑ Is there an additional security deposit (i.e., for specialty or custom items)?
❑ When is the final payment due?

Rental Checklist

Here is a checklist for the normal rental wedding items.

TABLES

- ❏ Bar
- ❏ Cake table
- ❏ Dessert or coffee table
- ❏ DJ (for equipment)
- ❏ Food service (prep, buffet, etc.)
- ❏ Gift table
- ❏ Guest tables
- ❏ Guestbook table
- ❏ Head table
- ❏ Place card table
- ❏ Sweetheart table

CHAIRS

- ❏ For the ceremony
- ❏ For the cocktail hour
- ❏ Highchair (for children)
- ❏ For the reception

LINENS

- ❏ Chair covers
- ❏ Linens for the tables you rent
- ❏ Napkins
- ❏ Overlays
- ❏ Table skirting

FOOD SERVICE/PLACE SETTINGS

- ❏ Bread plates
- ❏ Butter dishes
- ❏ Cake/dessert plates
- ❏ Cups and saucers
- ❏ Dinner plates
- ❏ Forks (salad, dinner, cake)
- ❏ Hors d'oeuvre plates
- ❏ Knives
- ❏ Salad plates
- ❏ Salt and pepper shakers

❏ Soup bowls
❏ Spoons (soup, dinner, coffee)
❏ Sugar and creamer sets

GLASSWARE
❏ Additional barware
❏ Bar glassware
❏ Champagne flutes
❏ Pitchers
❏ Specialty glasses (i.e., martini)
❏ Water glasses
❏ Wineglasses

MISCELLANEOUS
❏ Aisle runners
❏ Arches, gazebos, chuppahs, or columns (for ceremony)
❏ Caterer supplies (consult with your caterer for a complete list of their specific needs and what is included with their services/pricing)
❏ Ceremony sound system (consult with entertainment)
❏ Chafing dishes
❏ Dance floor
❏ Furniture (lounge chairs, sofas, coffee tables, etc.)
❏ Ice buckets and tubs
❏ Lighting (décor)
❏ Lighting (utilitarian)
❏ Podium or stand for officiant at ceremony
❏ Portable restrooms
❏ Potted plants/trees/shrubs
❏ Serving pieces
❏ Staging
❏ Tenting
❏ Trash cans

CHAPTER 16

Eat, Drink, and Be Married

*E*ating, drinking, and being merry is always in fashion. Thank goodness, since a major component of any wedding reception is the food and drink. It is also one of the largest chunks of the wedding budget. So, don't leave anything to chance with these major decisions. There are many options for creating a pleasing menu that suits the festivities. Explore your options and design a menu of food and beverage that will "wow" your guests.

Grilling the Caterer

Depending on your location, you may have to hire an outside caterer. A hotel or other wedding venue typically caters the meals; however, if you select on offsite venue, you will need to hire a caterer. No matter what type of caterer you work with, there are a number of key questions you should ask before making a commitment. Once you've found a caterer with all the right answers, get every part of your agreement in writing.

Catered Away

All caterers are not created equal; most tend to have a specialty or style. When shopping around, you'll be confronted with a variety of options so you'll need to know some basic facts to get you started. Here's the skinny on every caterer under the sun.

CATERING OPTIONS:

- In-house (Onsite) caterers are provided by or contracted exclusively by your reception site and are usually located on the premises. This is the type of service offered by all hotels and most country clubs. In-house caterers are already familiar with the particulars of the room and can offer a lot of suggestions. On the flip side, because of the "lack" of competition, their pricing may not be as competitive, and typically you must select a menu from what is within their abilities (most are well trained and can meet requests).

- Independent (Offsite) caterers come in all shapes and sizes. Your budget and needs will ultimately determine which style of food service and caterer is best for your event. Each offers a different degree of service so there's no reason to settle for anything less than sheer perfection. The following are the main types that you're likely to encounter:

  * **Food only.** These caterers specialize in keeping it simple—they provide food. You have to plan everything else. This type of service can save you money by allowing you to purchase the alcohol yourself to avoid the typical markups that usually accompany an open bar. However, you will invest time selecting and ordering rentals, hiring waitstaff, and working through the details on your own.

  * **Food and service.** This is the type of caterer that most people associate with a wedding reception. They provide the food, beverage, waitstaff, and bartenders, and will usually assist with arranging for rentals as they pertain to the wedding reception (china, glassware, tables, chairs, etc.). Of course, you will be paying for these extra services.

  * **All-inclusive.** These caterers offer just about every item and service you could possibly imagine, as well as a few you probably couldn't. Many have branched out into the event planning business. Basically, if you choose to pay them for it, you can spend the months before your wedding in worry-free bliss, and leave the reception planning to the caterer. The price tag is typically higher for this type of caterer, and you may have to work exclusively with their preferred vendor selections.

Questions to Ask

Following is a list of questions to ask potential caterers. Your questions will become more specific once you book a venue, but in general, the following questions apply to most caterers.

- ❏ What is your experience and catering background?
- ❏ Do you have packages for the meals or is everything priced separately?
- ❏ What is the final food price? (Caterers usually quote you an estimated price based on food prices at that time.)
- ❏ What types of meal service are offered? Sit-down? Buffet? Stations? Family style?
- ❏ What are my menu options? Do you have predetermined menus, or may I create my own? Do you specialize in any particular cuisine?
- ❏ When may we taste our selections? Is there a fee?
- ❏ Do you provide bar service?
- ❏ Is the catering service covered with proper insurance? (To protect yourself, make sure the caterer has the proper amount of liability insurance to cover property damage, bodily injury, and accidents that could occur after the wedding as a result of alcohol being served. Most venues require this and will not let the caterer work at the site without it.)
- ❏ What will the ratio of staff-to-guests be? Will there be enough people to serve the tables? Will the waitstaff be dressed appropriately for the occasion?
- ❏ Will they make provisions for guests with special dietary needs? (It's only proper that you plan ahead for guests on vegetarian, low-cholesterol, or kosher diets.)
- ❏ Will meals be provided for the disc jockey (or band), photographer, and videographer? What do you serve them and at what cost?
- ❏ What is the price difference between having hors d'oeuvres on display and having them served by the waitstaff?
- ❏ Can you provide a wedding cake? How about a dessert table?
- ❏ Is there a "cake-cutting fee"?
- ❏ Do you provide any rental items, such as linens, place settings, barware?
- ❏ Can you inspect rental items (linens, dinnerware, glassware)? Will you unpack and repack them for the rental company?

❑ How do you charge for the waitstaff's time? What about overtime?

❑ Does the caterer's fee include gratuities for the staff? If not, what is customary?

❑ What is the cancellation and refund policy?

❑ What does the caterer do with leftover food?

❑ Do you have references? (If you are not familiar with a caterer's work, ask for references.)

Caterer Checklist

Item	Description	Cost	Source (if not the caterer)
❑ Bartenders:			
❑ Beverages:			
❑ Cake:			
❑ Chairs:			
❑ Champagne:			
❑ Coat checkers:			
❑ Coffee service (specialty coffee bar):			
❑ Dessert:			
❑ Dinnerware:			
❑ Entrées:			
❑ Equipment:			
❑ Flatware:			
❑ Food:			
❑ Glassware:			
❑ Hors d'oeuvres:			
❑ Linens:			
❑ Liquor:			
❑ Nonalcoholic:			
❑ Servers:			
❑ Service (waitstaff):			
❑ Serving pieces:			
❑ Tables:			
❑ Tent:			
❑ Valet parking:			
❑ Wine:			
❑ Other:			

Let's Eat

The menu you select for the wedding meal should reflect the time of day and formality of the event. For example, a four-course plated meal suits a formal evening affair while a cake and hors d'oeuvres reception better suits an afternoon event. When it is time to plan the menu, consider all of the elements of the wedding to make the right selections.

Service Options

When it comes to meal service, you have options; however, particular venues and caterers may specialize in one style or another, and not all caterers and locations will be able to accommodate all of the options.

- The sit-down or plated meal is a traditional, usually more formal meal service. It involves at least three courses, a salad/soup/appetizer, an entrée, and a dessert. Other combinations include a salad/soup/appetizer, an intermezzo, and an entrée. Of course, many upscale locations offer four- and five-course meals as well. Make sure the venue/caterer has enough waitstaff to serve all the guests in a timely fashion.
- A buffet offers a display of food that guests can revisit as often as they like. Make sure that there are enough clean plates for multiple visits through the line, that the catering manager or emcee has a system for sending guests to the buffet to avoid long lines, and finally, that there are two or more buffet lines set up to avoid bottlenecking if it is a large wedding.
- Food stations that serve made-to-order dishes are a popular option. You can generally expect to have at least three stations set up around the venue, each offering specialties (sushi, pasta, salad, carving, etc.). Due to the labor involved (chefs on hand at each of the stations), this is one of the more costly options.
- Family-style meals are now being seen at formal and at casual weddings. The caterer serves dishes to the tables and the guests pass them around, serving themselves as if they were at your home.

Menu Checklist

When it is time to plan the reception menu, review the Menu Checklist to make sure you are not leaving out any necessities or niceties.

MENU CHECKLIST AND CONSIDERATIONS
- ❏ Bar
- ❏ Children's selection
- ❏ Coffee and/or tea
- ❏ Dessert
- ❏ Entrée
- ❏ First course
- ❏ Hors d'oeuvres
- ❏ Kosher options
- ❏ Nonalcoholic beverages
- ❏ Vegetarian selection
- ❏ Vegan selection

Menu Worksheet

A menu tasting can be overwhelming. You will be tasting a number of hors d'oeuvres and probably two to three entrées. Pay attention to the options that are being presented.

HORS D'OEUVRES
- Number of selections: _____
- Description/Opinion:

  _____
  _____
  _____
  _____
  _____
  _____

- Final selection:

  _____
  _____
  _____

FIRST COURSE
- Description/Opinion:

  _____
  _____
  _____

- Final selection:

  _____
  _____
  _____

SECOND COURSE
- Description/Opinion:
  _____
  _____
  _____

- Final selection:
  _____
  _____
  _____

ENTRÉE
- Description/Opinion
  _____
  _____
  _____

- Final selection:
  _____
  _____
  _____

DESSERT
- Description/Opinion:
  _____
  _____
  _____

- Final selection:
  _____
  _____
  _____

Stocking the Bar

You do not have to serve alcoholic beverages at a wedding. Just because someone expects something doesn't mean it is a necessity. You simply must provide the guests with refreshments, and nonalcoholic beverages are perfectly fine.

Bar Lingo
When the time comes to select the type of beverage service you would like, it is helpful to know the options that are available.

Consider your guest list, style of reception, and your budget to determine the style of beverage and/or bar service you will offer the guests.

FIRST DECISIONS:
- Open bar versus cash bar. There is no argument here. Your guests are your guests and should not be asked to pay for anything.
- A full bar provides a complete selection of alcoholic and non-alcoholic beverages. For example, guests will be able to select mixed drinks, wine, or sodas at their pleasure.
- A soft or limited bar provides nonalcoholic beverages. However, many soft bars now include beer and wine, lighter alcoholic fare.
- A dry house is a beverage service that does not serves alcohol.

Chances are good that the caterer will ask your preference on the quality of bar you would like to provide.

- A house bar consists of lower-priced brands the venue or caterer typically serves.
- A premium bar is stocked with higher-end brand-name selections.
- A deluxe or top-shelf bar serves top-of-the-line liquor.

Bar Options
The following suggestions are some of the more popular ways couples "stock their bars." Select a beverage plan that fits your budget and review and discuss it with your caterer and/or location manager to formulate a plan that works for everyone involved.

- Serve a sparkling wine instead of champagne.
- Rather than serving champagne or sparkling wine for the toasts, let guests toast with what they are already drinking.
- If you know your guests are not drinkers or you are having a weekday or morning wedding when alcohol consumption is usually less, have a consumption bar (where you pay per drink) rather than purchasing the site's bar package.
- If you are offering hard liquor, offer house brands rather than premium brands.
- Serve a champagne punch, as it is fairly light in terms of alcohol, and people aren't likely to pound down glass after glass.

- Try a fully stocked open bar for the first hour of the reception. Then switch to a soft bar with wine and beer and nonalcoholic drinks.
- Try an open bar for the first hour of the reception. This will get things off on the right foot and many brides feel this fulfills their responsibility. This is a popular "trend," but strictly speaking, breaks the laws of etiquette.

Sweet Stuff

The cake has become a highlight of the wedding reception. Modern couples are taking cakes to the next level with unique designs and gourmet flavors. Pick your favorite and enjoy a sweet moment with your new husband.

Cake 101

Each baker will have his or her repertoire of flavors—chocolate to tiramisu—and fillings—fresh fruit to white chocolate ganache. Before you get to that point, you need to know a little about cake and icing options.

CAKE STYLES
- **Pillar.** Each tier of the cake is separated by pillars (clear, white, colored, etc.). The space between the pillars may remain empty or may be accented with flowers
- **Stacked.** This cake is stacked one tier on top of the other, with no space showing between the layers.
- **Cascade** or **satellite.** Each layer is decorated separately and placed upon its own pedestal, which stands independently of the others. The pedestals are of varying heights so that it appears the individual cakes are cascading.

THE ICING:
- **Fondant.** A smooth sheetlike icing that is rolled out, fondant gives a smooth clean look and is very popular with the very modern and intricate styles of cakes today.
- **Butter cream.** A creamy sweet icing that is a traditional favorite, butter cream can be flavored and spread on smoothly, but it does not give the "sharp" or defined smooth look that fondant gives.

To finish off the look of the wedding cake, depending on your budget and the skill level of the professional you hire, you will be able to select from a variety of shapes. Hexagons, squares, and even dragons are the norm. The cake can be finished off with fresh flowers, sugar flowers, and other adornments crafted from edible and nonedible materials.

Just for Him

Some weddings also feature a groom's cake, traditionally a dark fruitcake packed into white boxes and given to the guests as a gift. Couples who opt for a groom's cake often have the cake decorated to resemble the groom's hobby or special interest. If your groom is a baseball fan, you might decide to have the cake shaped like a bat or a ball. Usually, the same baker makes both the wedding cake and the groom's cake.

Cake Shopping

Wedding cakes today are no simple affair; they may require a small army of bakers (and large chunks of time and money) to put together. Couples take great pleasure in designing edible masterpieces to display at their wedding. To get moving on your cake selections, here's what you're going to have to do:

- Begin searching for a bakery at least six months before the wedding, possibly longer if you are looking for an intricate or specialty design
- Bring in examples from magazines, photos, or books to show the cake designer, or view the bakery's sample books to find the right cake for you
- Ask for taste tests of any style cake you're seriously considering
- Tell the baker how many guests you expect
- Find out how much of a deposit is required
- Find out if the deposit is refundable
- Ask about any additional delivery or rental charges
- Ask whether there will be a fee for having the baker set up the cake at the reception site
- Arrange when final payment for the cake is due
- Order the cake
- Get a written contract stipulating the type of cake, cost, date of delivery, and any other important specifications

- Arrange for the baker to arrive at the reception site before the guests to set up the cake
- Decide where the cake will be displayed

Questions to Ask

With so many options, coming to a final decision can be pretty hard. Here's a list of questions to ask your baker.

❏ What size cake should you have for the number of guests you're having?

❏ Can you have different flavors for different layers of the cake?

❏ When do you make your cakes? Are they made and then frozen or are the cakes fresh?

❏ What are the ingredients you typically use? (This may be important if you are looking for a specific kind of cake such as organic, vegan, etc.)

❏ What choices are available in cake flavors and frostings?

❏ Does the baker specialize in any flavor, style, or size?

❏ Do you offer a cake tasting? Is there a charge?

❏ Is there a rental fee for tiers or separators?

CAKE WORKSHEET

Bakery name: _____

Address: _____

Phone: _____

Contact: _____

Cake Flavors: _____ Cost: _____

_____ Cost: _____

_____ Cost: _____

Icing (frosting): _____

Number of tiers: _____

Ornaments: _____

Samples: _____

Notes: _____

_____

_____

Preserving the Top Layer

Traditionally, the bride and groom preserve the top tier of their wedding cake to eat on their first anniversary. Check with your bakery, because some bakeries will now provide a small cake on your first anniversary in lieu of your freezing your top tier. However, if you want to save the original cake, refrigeration alone isn't going to cut it. Taking the following measures should ensure that you'll have an edible cake on your first anniversary:

- Wrap it tightly in plastic
- Place it in a sturdy box
- Wrap it in plastic again
- Store it in the freezer
- When the time to eat your cake is here, thaw it in the wrappings for approximately twelve hours, then simply unwrap and enjoy!

CHAPTER 17

Places, Please

*A*s the producer of your wedding extravaganza, it is also your job to make sure everyone knows where to go, when to go, and what to do. The rehearsal is your opportunity to iron out last-minute details and resolve any remaining questions. Though it may not be enough to truly calm your nerves, getting the details straight at the rehearsal is your chance to make sure that everything is ready and all of the participants know what's expected of them.

Let's Practice

For things to flow smoothly on your wedding day a well-orchestrated rehearsal is necessary. Usually held the evening before the wedding (it can also be held a day or two before or during the daytime) at the ceremony location, it is a time for everyone involved to become familiar themselves with the venue and participate in a run-through of the ceremony.

What to Expect

The officiant or wedding planner will do a quick run-through of the ceremony from processional to recessional, making sure that the wedding party and parents know their positions and seats, ushers learn all their duties, reader's practice their readings, and soloists run through their pieces.

Afterward, don't forget to review any special rules the venue may have. Pass out the itinerary to everyone and include directions to the rehearsal dinner—they are bound to ask!

Rehearsal Location _____

Address: _____

Officiant: _____

Wedding Coordinator (for venue): _____

Phone: _____

Date: _____

Time: _____

Who Should Be There

Now it is time to plan the rehearsal. Make sure those who should attend know they are expected. The following list should help.

- Bride
- Groom
- Bride's attendants
- Bride's parents
- Candle lighters
- Child attendants (flower girl, ring bearer, pages)
- Godparents (optional)
- Grandparents (optional)
- Groom's attendants
- Groom's parents
- Officiant (in most cases, but not always)
- Readers
- Soloists
- Ushers
- Wedding planner

Orchestrating the Rehearsal

Prepare for the rehearsal by deciding on the following points (finalize the information on the Rehearsal Worksheet).

- In what order will the attendants enter and leave?
- Where will the attendants stand for the ceremony?
- Will the grandparents be formally seated? If so, by whom?
- Who will seat the groom's mother?
- Who will seat the bride's mother?
- If there are stepparents, will they be involved in any part of the ceremony?
- From where will the readers speak, and in what order?

The Rehearsal Worksheet

Once you've organized your thoughts, use this Rehearsal Worksheet to finalize the details.

Seating

Groom's grandparents: _____ Seated by: _____
Bride's grandparents: _____ Seated by: _____
Groom's mother: _____ Seated by: _____
Bride's mother: _____ Seated by: _____

Processional (list in order from closest to the bride/groom to farthest away.):

_____
_____
_____
_____
_____
_____

Maid of honor: _____ Best man: _____
Flower girl: _____ Ring bearer: _____
Bridesmaids: Groomsmen:

_____
_____
_____
_____
_____
_____

The Ceremony (run through whichever components are applicable)

Processional
Opening words
Giving away or blessing
Reading #1: _____ by: _____
Reading #2: _____ by: _____
Solo: _____ by: _____
Prayers
Marriage vows
Exchange of rings

Pronouncement of marriage
Lighting of unity candle
Benediction
Closing words
Recessional (opposite order of processional, maid of honor and best man lead off after the couple)

_____
_____
_____
_____
_____
_____
_____

What to Bring

If possible, arrange to leave some of the essential wedding day items at the ceremony venue so you won't have to worry about bringing them to the ceremony. Don't leave any money, payments, or your marriage license—hand that to the best man, wedding planner, or a trusted friend. (Hint: Make the same arrangements with the reception venue.)

- Aisle runner
- Fee for officiant
- Fee for site
- Flower girl basket
- Itineraries
- Maps or written directions
- Marriage license
- Practice bouquet
- Ring pillow
- Unity candles
- Wedding day transportation information
- Wedding programs

Eat and Drink . . . Before You Marry

The rehearsal dinner is a time for the people involved in the wedding to enjoy some special time before the big day. Rehearsal dinners don't need to be dinners at all; luncheons are perfectly acceptable. The timing will be dictated by the time of the wedding rehearsal.

Rehearsal Dinner Location
Party location: _____
Address: _____
Contact person: _____
Phone: _____
Time: _____

Planning the Dinner

A rehearsal dinner can be formal or casual. The one thing it should not do, in size or formality, is eclipse the actual wedding. Watch the size of your guest list and take into account the events of the wedding day. For example, if you are planning a casual barbecue for the wedding, a four-course rehearsal dinner would be out-of-place.

Traditionally, the expense of the rehearsal party is borne by the groom's parents, but these days anyone who wishes may sponsor the party. Typically an informal affair, the rehearsal party usually takes place in a restaurant or a private home; a simple phone call is the usual means of inviting the guests. E-mail or traditional invitations may be used as well.

Having a good time is the only thing that is required at the rehearsal dinner. Often couples will use this opportunity to present the attendants and their parents with thank-you gifts. This is the time to have personal toasts and lots of them . . . if you wish.

Guess Who's Coming to Dinner?

Strictly speaking, the following people should be invited:

- ❏ All members of the wedding party, along with their spouses or significant others (and children, if applicable)
- ❏ The parents of the bride and groom
- ❏ Siblings of the bride and groom
- ❏ The ceremony officiant, along with his or her spouse or significant other
- ❏ Children in the wedding party and their parents
- ❏ Readers, soloists, who were expected to be at the rehearsal
- ❏ Grandparents of the bride and groom
- ❏ Godparents of the bride and groom
- ❏ Out-of-town wedding guests (if money and space permit, inviting out-of-town guests is a nice gesture but not required)

❑   Any special friends and family members, again if money and
     space permits

Of course, you can invite anyone else you want, but try to keep
the party intimate. Remember, the goal is to allow everyone to relax
and to give you and your groom some additional time with loved ones
who may only be in town for a few days. You'll have plenty of time to
party with your other wedding guests on the big day.

Tokens of Appreciation

As you planned your wedding, many people provided an ear, lent a
hand, and were simply willing to listen to you go on about bridesmaids' dresses or ivory roses. Now is the time to show your gratitude.

Attendants' Gifts

Bestowing gifts upon your wedding attendants is the most popular way to say thank-you for all the work, time, and money these kind
souls have put into your wedding. Although it's common to give all
the bridesmaids and groomsmen the same gift to avoid resentment
or hurt feelings, you can always individualize a little. These tokens of
appreciation are disbursed during the rehearsal dinner, so you have
some time to find just the right items. The following are some popular
gift ideas:

FOR THE BRIDESMAIDS:
- Jewelry (possibly something they can wear for the wedding such
  as earrings or a bracelet)
- Date book
- Stationery
- Perfume
- Beauty product gift pack
- Jewelry box
- Monogrammed purse mirrors
- Gift card (to a favorite store or spa)
- Something related to a favorite hobby of the bridesmaid

FOR THE GROOMSMEN:
- Monogrammed money clip or key chain
- Date book

- Pen set
- Cologne
- Silk tie
- Travel or shaving kit
- Gift certificate (to a sporting goods store, for instance)
- Tickets to a favorite sporting event or concert
- Something related to a favorite hobby of the groomsman

Thanks, Mom and Dad!

Your parents have raised and loved you. They may have helped pay for your wedding or at least provided some guidance and assistance. Thank them appropriately, too.

FOR THE PARENTS:

- Flowers
- A commemorative tree (to plant in their yard)
- Tickets to a play/concert/sporting event
- Gift card to a favorite store
- Gift card to a favorite restaurant
- His/hers spa package
- An invitation to a gourmet dinner prepared by you and your husband, in your new home, on your new china

CHAPTER 18

Countdown to the Wedding Day!

That magical day that seemed as though it was so far away is right around the corner. You've planned, you've confirmed, you've planned some more. All that's left to do is get married, or so it seems. As you prepare for the wedding day, a little reorganization is in order. Review the details and logistics, call your vendors, and create an itinerary. If possible, schedule some couple time, too. Before you know it, the pieces will fall into place, and your vision will come to life.

Tying Up Loose Ends

You've done the work, but how do you make sense of it all? How do you get everyone to the right places at the right times? How do you make sure your carefully laid plans are executed? It can be overwhelming, but with an itinerary and some vendor follow-up, you are on the road to bliss!

The Itinerary

The itinerary is a timeline of the wedding day events. It outlines the who, what, when, and where of the important places and events for the people involved in the wedding. If you have a wedding planner, he or she will put together the itinerary for you. If not, you need to work with the venue and vendors to put the itinerary together. Make copies of the itinerary and pass them out to the wedding party, families, readers, soloists, and any other people helping at the wedding.

Itinerary Checklist

The following steps highlight the information you should include in your wedding day itinerary.

CREATING AN ITINERARY

- ❑ Begin with the established start times of the ceremony and reception, and work forward and backward to fill in the schedule.
- ❑ Confirm arrival and setup times with the ceremony and/or reception venues.
- ❑ Schedule departure and arrival times, accounting for travel time to and from all locations.
- ❑ Schedule preceremony events, such as hair and makeup and photo sessions.
- ❑ Confirm arrival and departure times with the vendors.
- ❑ Create a schedule for photography (work with the photographer).
- ❑ Determine which traditions will be incorporated into the ceremony and reception.
- ❑ Confirm and review the timing for the formalities (grand entrance, toast, first dance, etc.) with the location manager and the entertainment.
- ❑ Include detailed information on décor and setup plan.
- ❑ Include contact names and office and cell phone numbers for all vendors.
- ❑ Include an emergency contact number (it should not be the bride). If you have a wedding planner, list her cell phone and office number. If not, give a friend the important vendor and logistical information, and list him as the contact.

Two Weeks to Go: Countdown Checklist

Although you've probably taken care of all the details by this time, it never hurts to double-check. Many of the following tasks may be (and probably should be) taken care of just before your wedding. Of course, if you try to accomplish them all up to a week before the wedding, you'll have more opportunity to relax and enjoy your last week of single life.

COUNTDOWN CHECKLIST

❏ Make sure the following people know the correct locations and times.

- Baker
- Band/DJ
- Ceremony site coordinator
- Florist
- Hairstylist
- Limousine/Transportation
- Makeup stylist
- Officiant
- Photographer
- Reception site coordinator
- Rentals
- Videographer

❏ Reconfirm your honeymoon travel arrangements and hotel reservations.

❏ Reconfirm your hotel reservation for your wedding night.

❏ Make sure your wedding attendants know where they need to be and when, and remind them of any special duties they need to perform.

❏ Finish any last-minute packing.

❏ Pack your going-away outfit and accessories. If you'll be changing at the reception site, put a trusted friend in charge of making sure they arrive there safely.

❏ Give your wedding rings and marriage license to your honor attendants to hold until the ceremony (at the rehearsal).

❏ Make sure your groom and best man have enough cash for tipping.

❏ Pack an "emergency kit."

❏ Make sure your honeymoon luggage is stored in the trunk of your "getaway car" or is sent ahead to wherever you're spending your wedding night.

❏ Arrange for a friend to drive your car to the reception site if you intend to drive yourselves to the hotel or inn where you'll be staying.

Making a List and Checking It Twice

After planning so carefully and spending so much money to create the perfect wedding day, now is not the time to let details slip. As the day draws nearer, call and e-mail each vendor to finalize details, including the wedding day itinerary.

Follow-Up

For these final correspondences with your vendors, speak with the vendor and have written confirmation as well. Use the following simple steps to be sure you have not skipped a beat.

- ❑ Supply each vendor with a copy of the itinerary (when necessary).
- ❑ Give each vendor directions to the ceremony/reception venue.
- ❑ Call each vendor to confirm receipt of the itinerary and to go over timing, and any questions or special requests.
- ❑ If you make any changes, get written confirmation.

Paperwork and Payments

Review your signed vendor contracts and paperwork. Use the following checklist to track when each vendor needs payment and any necessary paperwork. Most vendors require final payments about two weeks before the day. Check your contracts to verify payment dates and how each vendor requests payment.

✎ PAYMENT AND PAPERWORK CHECKLIST

Vendor	Payment Due	Payment Sent	Paperwork Sent
		❑	❑
		❑	❑
		❑	❑
		❑	❑
		❑	❑
		❑	❑
		❑	❑
		❑	❑
		❑	❑

Vendor	Payment Due	Payment Sent	Paperwork Sent
		❏	❏
		❏	❏
		❏	❏
		❏	❏
		❏	❏
		❏	❏

Packing for the Big Day

It's almost here . . . the *big* day is right around the corner! Your dreams are coming to life. So, prepare an emergency kit, get the bridesmaids and groomsmen ready . . . and pack those wedding accessories . . . it is finally time to use them!

The Bridal Emergency Kit Checklist

A wedding day emergency kit includes simple everyday items, as well as wedding-specific items. You never know when a guest might need some antacid or some aspirin or a bridesmaid's stocking will run.

BRIDAL EMERGENCY KIT
- ❏ Aspirin or Ibuprofen
- ❏ Baby or talcum powder
- ❏ Bobby pins
- ❏ White-Out (last resort for covering up stains on a wedding dress)
- ❏ Bottled water
- ❏ Breath mints
- ❏ Cellophane tape
- ❏ Clean sheet for the bride to dress (Placing a sheet on the floor for the bride to stand on while dressing helps to avoid getting excess dirt and dust on her gown)
- ❏ Clean white cloth (for cleaning stains on a wedding dress)
- ❏ Clear bandages or liquid bandage
- ❏ Clear nail polish
- ❏ Corsage pins

- ❏ Crackers, energy bars, etc.
- ❏ Deodorant
- ❏ Double-stick tape
- ❏ Duct tape (one regular and one in white)
- ❏ Extra stockings
- ❏ Facial tissue or handkerchief
- ❏ Glue (super glue, hot glue, and hot glue gun)
- ❏ Hairspray
- ❏ Money
- ❏ Mouthwash
- ❏ Nail glue
- ❏ Nail polish (to match your shade for a quick touchup)
- ❏ Rubber bands
- ❏ Sanitary napkins/tampons
- ❏ Scissors
- ❏ Sewing kit (including straight pins, needle, and thread—white and black thread as well as a color to match the bridesmaid's dresses and the groomsmen's accessories)
- ❏ Spot remover
- ❏ Static cling spray
- ❏ Toothbrush and toothpaste
- ❏ Tweezers
- ❏ White chalk (for concealing dirt smudges)

Wedding Day Accessories

Following is a checklist of wedding day accessories. Keep in mind, that this is a generic checklist. Your particular wedding may have more accessories or fewer, as well as other specialty items, just add them in, check them off, and you are ready for the wedding day.

WEDDING ACCESSORY CHECKLIST

- ❏ Aisle runner
- ❏ Bubbles, rose petals, etc. (for tossing or send off)
- ❏ Cake knife and server
- ❏ Cake topper
- ❏ Cash and envelopes (for last-minute tips and expenses)
- ❏ Card box (for gift table)
- ❏ Centerpieces
- ❏ Copies of itinerary, vendor contracts, vendor contact numbers, seating chart

- ❑ Decorations
- ❑ Disposable cameras for each table
- ❑ Engagement photos
- ❑ Favors
- ❑ Flower girl basket
- ❑ Guest book
- ❑ Guest list (alphabetized with seating arrangements)
- ❑ Pens for guest book
- ❑ Place cards
- ❑ Ring pillow
- ❑ Table numbers
- ❑ Toasting flutes
- ❑ Unity candle
- ❑ Wedding programs

CHAPTER 19

The Trip of a Lifetime

With all the frenzied coordinating, organizing, and worrying involved, getting yourself married can be a full-time job—and then some! When it's all over, you'll need more than just an ordinary vacation to recuperate. On the surface, a honeymoon is no different from any other vacation you might take, but to newlyweds, the honeymoon is a much-anticipated getaway. This once-in-a-lifetime trip is the grand finale of your wedding, and the reward for your careful planning.

Decisions! Decisions!

Some of the most sought-after destinations may be booked up to a year in advance, so begin your planning early and don't get locked into what you think a honeymoon has to be. A honeymoon can be anything you want from backpacking across Europe to lounging on a beach in the Caribbean to camping in the mountains.

Where to Go

Working with a qualified and knowledgeable travel agent is the key to honeymoon success. Just as you were diligent with your wedding professionals, use these same practices when finding a travel agent. He or she can steer you toward the right destinations for your interests and offer up-to-the-minute advice about traveling and vacationing.

Before you book your honeymoon, research the destination and surrounding areas carefully. Consider travel advisories, political situations, and even what the weather conditions have been over the last year or so. Then check into travel documentation or immunizations you may need. Once you decide, purchase a local guidebook to start planning the trip and making notes on points of interest.

If you will be flying, make travel arrangements for your honeymoon under your maiden name. You will not have a passport or driver's license in your married name yet, and you must be able to present the proper documentation to travel.

Saver's Fares

While perusing through your honeymoon options, you might find that your budget has as much of an impact on your final destination as your dreams. Great deals are available—provided you do a little research. If you are trying to save money or are on a tight budget, look for special air/hotel package deals, low-price airfares, and consider alternative accommodations, such as house/apartment swaps, hostels, or a bed-and-breakfast instead of a luxury hotel.

Here is a list of places to consult for potentially inexpensive travel arrangements.

- Travel agents
- Internet travel sites
- Travel books
- Travel magazines
- Travel section of the newspaper
- Travel blogs

Making the Trip

To be sure you can relax and enjoy your honeymoon, take these simple steps to ensure that your home is safe.

Final Prep

You are almost there . . . just a few more things to do:

- ❑ Go to the bank for money, traveler's checks
- ❑ Double-check travel advisories
- ❑ Go through the packing list

- ❑ Gather your travel documents
- ❑ Make sure you have TSA-approved luggage locks
- ❑ Book or confirm airport transportation
- ❑ Arrange with your mom or maid of honor to drop off any rentals, ship your bouquet (to be preserved), and deliver your dress (to the preservationist)
- ❑ Confirm your honeymoon details including the following:
    - ❑ Call the airline to check flights, restrictions on luggage and carry-ons, security alerts, seat reservations, and special meal requests
    - ❑ Confirm reservations with the hotel
    - ❑ Confirm the rental car

Holding Down the Fort

Although you are on your honeymoon, back home life marches on. Make arrangements to protect your home, and you will have no worries while you are away, relaxing and enjoying each other's company.

- ❑ Hire a house sitter or ask a neighbor to "watch over" the place while you are gone
- ❑ Hire a pet sitter
- ❑ Have your mail held
- ❑ Have packages held or redirected to your parents, to a neighbor, or to a close friend

Travel Tips

Tipping often presents embarrassing and confusing questions when you travel. In some situations, you can ask your companions at the dining table in a hotel or on ship or the management, but it's better to understand the travel tipping structure.

TIPPING AT THE AIRPORT

- **The porter:** $1 per bag when you check in at the curb or have bags taken to check in for you. If the luggage is heavy, tip a little more. Obviously, if you go the DIY route, no tip is necessary or expected.

HOTELS AND RESORTS

- **Bellboy:** $1 per bag, plus $1 for hospitable gestures, such as turning on lights, opening windows. Tip on service.
- **Chambermaid:** $1 for each service, minimum $5 per couple per week. Tip each day; a new chambermaid may be assigned during your stay.
- **Doorman:** $1 per bag; $1 for hailing a taxi. Tip on service.
- **Headwaiter:** $5 per week for special service, $2–$3 for regular service—tip on your first day.
- **Waitstaff:** 15–20 percent of the bill when no service charge is added; some add 5 percent when there is a service charge. Tip at each meal.
- **Room Service:** 15–20 percent of bill in addition to room service charge. If the menu or bill explicitly states that a gratuity will automatically be added, you might add an additional $1 or refrain from tipping altogether.
- **Other service personnel:** the general rule to follow is to tip 15–20 percent of the bill, unless the person serving you owns the business.

TIPPING ON CRUISE SHIPS

The staff on each cruise line can outline tipping etiquette and procedures for their ship. Some ships are "no-tip" ships, some automatically add a gratuity to the bill, and others practice person-to-person tipping (each staff person is presented with an envelope on the last night of the cruise).

- **Room steward:** Tip: $3.50 per day per person. Tip at the end of the trip.
- **Dining room waiter and busboy:** Waiter, $3.50 per person per day, half that for the busboy.
- **Bartenders, wine steward, pool and deck attendants:** On almost all ships, a service charge is automatically added to the bar bill, making a tip unnecessary. Be sure to check.
- **Other service personnel:** should be tipped when the service is given, at the same rate as for service ashore, usually 15 percent.
- **Maitre d', headwaiter:** Seventy-five cents per day, per guest.

Pack Your Bags!

Don't get caught running around the house in your wedding gown, throwing clothes into suitcases while your ride to the airport waits. It would be great if you could pack for your trip a week beforehand, but that's probably unrealistic. However, if use the following checklist and begin packing early, you should be able to simplify the process.

Packing Checklist

Haste can make for forgetfulness, so plan well and plan early. Use the Packing Checklist to keep you on track.

IN YOUR CARRY-ON BAG:

- ❏ Airline tickets
- ❏ A complete travel itinerary (with hotel and rental car information and confirmation numbers as well as contact numbers for the travel agent)
- ❏ Medications
- ❏ Birth control
- ❏ Driver's licenses or legal (approved) valid photo identification
- ❏ Eyewear
- ❏ Foreign currency and/or traveler's checks
- ❏ List of credit card numbers
- ❏ List of luggage contents (for insurance purposes if the luggage is lost or stolen)
- ❏ Name and phone number of someone to contact in case of emergency
- ❏ Passports or visas (if appropriate)
- ❏ Proof of age and citizenship
- ❏ Vaccination certificates (if necessary)
- ❏ Valuable jewelry

TOILETRIES

- ❏ Deodorant
- ❏ Eyeglasses/Contacts/Contact lens solution
- ❏ Hair care products
- ❏ Insect repellent
- ❏ Lingerie
- ❏ Cosmetics and beauty care
- ❏ Perfume or cologne

❏ Razors/Shaving cream/Aftershave
❏ Soap and skin care products
❏ Sun screen
❏ Toothbrush/Toothpaste/Dental care products
❏ Vitamins

ACCESSORIES
❏ Backpack
❏ Camera and extra memory cards (or film)
❏ Electrical adapter (if necessary)
❏ Hats
❏ Sunglasses
❏ Umbrellas
❏ Video camera
❏ Waist pouch

FOR THE BEACH
❏ Bathing suits
❏ Sandals
❏ Cover-ups
❏ Sunscreen and tanning lotion
❏ Sunglasses
❏ Beach bag

FOR THE SNOW
❏ Winter jacket
❏ Hats
❏ Boots
❏ Gloves
❏ Sweaters
❏ Thick socks
❏ Skis (if you have them)

CHAPTER 20

Beyond the Wedding

*B*elieve it or not, the day will come when you wake up a married woman and no longer have a wedding to plan. That, however, does not mean you are off the hook. After all the months you spent planning, you must still dedicate a little more of your precious time to taking care of some remaining details like changing your name, writing thank-you notes, and figuring out exactly what you are going to do with all this stuff. Oh yeah, by the way . . . congratulations! Now go on and enjoy married life!

The Name Game

For years, you may have taken your surname for granted, but faced with its possible loss, you may find yourself more attached to the name than you'd realized. This is the name you went through school with, the name you went to work with, the name everyone knows you by. It feels like a part of you. On the other hand, maybe your last name is ten syllables long, or no one can ever pronounce or spell it right, and you can't wait to get rid of it.

Options

When it comes time to a decision on your name, there are options. Here's the scoop on getting it done.

- Use your maiden name as your middle name and your husband's as your last. So if Jennifer Andrews married Trevor Miller, she'd be Jennifer Andrews Miller.

- Hyphenate the two last names: Jennifer Andrews-Miller. This means that the two separate last names are now joined to make one name (kind of like a marriage). You keep your regular middle name, but saying your full name can be a mouthful: Jennifer Marie Andrews-Miller.
- Take your husband's name legally, but use your maiden name professionally. In everyday life and social situations, you'd use your married name; but in the office, you'd use the same name you always had.
- Hyphenate both your and your husband's last names: Jennifer Andrews-Miller and Richard Andrews-Miller.

Make it Legal

Before you can make any official changes to you name, you will need to have your official marriage license. Once that is in hand, you can download forms from the Internet (or pick them up/request them via mail or phone). You will need a new social security card and a legally valid form of identification, usually a driver's license.

One easy way to tackle this task is with a name change kit. These kits are widely available and provide the proper forms and information you need legally to change your name. Each state has its own requirements, so be sure to purchase a kit that is customized for your state.

NAME CHANGE DOCUMENT CHECKLIST

- ❏ Bank accounts (savings, checking, 401k plans, investment accounts, etc.)
- ❏ Car registrations
- ❏ Credit cards
- ❏ Driver's license
- ❏ Employment records
- ❏ Insurance policies
- ❏ Internal Revenue Service records
- ❏ Leases
- ❏ Passport
- ❏ Pension plan records
- ❏ Post office listings
- ❏ Property titles
- ❏ School records or alumni listings

- ❏ Social security
- ❏ Stock certificates
- ❏ Utility and telephone information
- ❏ Voter registration
- ❏ Will

Thank You

Thank-you notes are one rule of etiquette that's here to stay. While everyone appreciates the gift, writing thank-you notes is not usually a favorite occupation. Ironically in today's world of instant communication, you are still expected to send a handwritten thank-you note every time you receive a gift.

What to Say

Thank-you notes for any shower gifts should be (or should have been!) sent within a few weeks of receiving the gift. For wedding gifts received prior to the wedding, you can thank-you notes as soon as you receive the gift. Just be sure to sign your maiden name to any thank-you cards written before you're married. For gifts received at or after the wedding, write your thank-you notes as soon as possible, within a month or two.

Really, thank-you notes are pretty simple. Here is what to include:

- ❏ Mention the gift
- ❏ Make a brief statement about how you plan to use it
- ❏ Thank the guest for his or her generosity.

Here are a couple of samples to help get you started.

Thank-You Note for a Wedding Gift

Dear Lynn and Dennis,

Thank you so much for the place setting of formal china. We really look forward to enjoying a lovely meal on our beautiful tableware during your next visit. We are so glad you were able to be with us at our wedding.

Fondly,

Christine

Thank-You Note for a Monetary Gift

Dear Barbara and Art,

Thank you so much for the generous gift. It will truly help us in completing our set of formal china. We appreciate your thoughtfulness. We are so glad you were able to be with us at our wedding.

Fondly,

Christine

Oh, the Memories

Two very sentimental items from a bride's wedding day are her gown and her bouquet. Whether you choose to keep them is entirely up to you. If you wish to preserve these special mementos, check into your options early.

Parting with the Gown

Keeping or not keeping your gown is a very personal decision. Whatever you decide, the gown needs to be cleaned. Here are a few ways brides part with their gowns.

- Sell the gown, either through a local consignment shop or on the Internet. Keep in mind this may not be an easy process; it has been altered and worn, and the value has dropped significantly, so don't expect to get a huge return on your investment.
- Donate your gown to a local charitable thrift shop.
- Donate your gown to a local or national organization that sells gently used (and new) gowns to help make wishes come true for breast cancer patients.
- Donate your gown to a fashion school, local college, or high school.

Keeping the Gown

If you want to keep and treasure this precious garment "forever," professional gown preservation is a must. Look into preserving it before the wedding; however, although it is not ideal, you can do it after the honeymoon.

With preserving, the gown will be cleaned, removing stains and repairing minor tears and damages, as well as beading and lacework.

Look for a gown preservation company that uses pH neutral, acid-free paper and containers. You should be able to remove your gown from the box to inspect it. Finally, work with a company that guarantees their services.

The Bouquet

Many brides choose to preserve their bridal bouquet as a memento of the wedding. Whether this is done professionally or is more of a DIY project does not really matter. If you want to keep it, do a little research to ensure you get the outcome you desire.

Professional Services

Professionally preserving your bouquet is not inexpensive. You will need to make arrangements ahead of time, as the instructions and shipping information must be in hand prior to the wedding day. Once the instructions arrive, read them carefully so you will know how to handle the bouquet after the ceremony. The bouquet should be on its way to the preservation company in the special shipping container on the first business day following your wedding. Ask your mother or maid of honor to be in charge of this task for you.

DIY Preservation

If professionally preserving your bouquet is out of the question or out of the budget, here are some DIY alternatives to preserve these special flowers.

Pressing

This is one of the most popular means of bouquet preservation. The process works best when it's started soon after the wedding, because the flowers have had less time to wilt. (If you ask nicely and promise to return the favor, you may be able to convince your maid of honor to do it while you're on your honeymoon.) Here are the steps to preserve your bouquet:

- Take a picture of your bouquet; you'll need it to refer to later.
- Take the bouquet apart (and that's no typo).
- Place the separate flowers in the pages of heavy books, between sheets of blank white paper (if you don't cushion the flowers with blank paper, ink from the book's pages will ruin them).

- Keep the flowers in the books for two to six weeks, depending on their size (the bigger the flower, the more time it will need).
- When the flowers look ready, glue them onto a mounting board in an arrangement that closely resembles the original bouquet in the photo.
- Place the board in a picture frame.
- Hang it wherever your heart desires.

Hanging/Drying

As with pressing, the earlier you start the process, the more successful it's likely to be. Here are the steps:

- Take a photo for future reference.
- Take the bouquet apart.
- Hang the flowers upside down to dry, thereby preventing drooping and keeping their shape (some color may be lost in the drying process, but this can be averted if the flowers are hung in a dark room).
- When the flowers are completely dry, spray them with shellac or silica gel for protection.
- Reassemble the flowers to match the photo.

Potpourri

This is a novel take on preserving the bridal bouquet; it involves tearing the whole thing apart. In the end, however, you'll never have to be without a little piece of your wedding.

- Buy some netting or lacy fabric.
- Buy some thin ribbon.
- Cut the netting into 4-inch squares.
- Dry the flowers.
- Gather the petals together.
- Place small piles of the petals into the 4-inch squares of netting.
- Tie the squares into little pouches with the ribbon.
- Place these little sachets anywhere you wish to fill the air with a small reminder of your wedding day.

Index

We Have
EVERYTHING®
on Anything!

With more than 19 million copies sold, the Everything® series has become one of America's favorite resources for solving problems, learning new skills, and organizing lives. Our brand is not only recognizable—it's also welcomed.

The series is a hand-in-hand partner for people who are ready to tackle new subjects—like you!

For more information on the Everything® series, please visit *www.adamsmedia.com*

The Everything® list spans a wide range of subjects, with more than 500 titles covering 25 different categories:

Business	History	Reference
Careers	Home Improvement	Religion
Children's Storybooks	Everything Kids	Self-Help
Computers	Languages	Sports & Fitness
Cooking	Music	Travel
Crafts and Hobbies	New Age	Wedding
Education/Schools	Parenting	Writing
Games and Puzzles	Personal Finance	
Health	Pets	